# Human Design
## Gate Strengths

### A Unique Synthesis & Reference Guide for the Human Design Gates

## JAMIE L. PALMER

Ecocentric
HD Press
Newport, RI

Human Design Gate Strengths

Published in Newport, RI, by Ecocentric HD Press.
Ecocentric HD Press is a Trademark of Jamie L. Palmer Consulting LLC

First Edition 2024
ISBN - 979-8-9905926-0-5

*For those who are ready to get back to the nature of who they are and are ready to embrace life at the intersection of their design, desires and lifestyle.*

# TABLE OF CONTENTS

**How To Use This Book** .................................................. 08

**Gate 1** - The Original .................................................. 12

**Gate 2** - The Visionary .................................................. 14

**Gate 3** - The Innovator .................................................. 16

**Gate 4** – The Solution Provider .................................................. 18

**Gate 5** - The Consistent Dependable .................................................. 20

**Gate 6** – The Big Family Or Multi-Preneur .................................................. 22

**Gate 7** – The Right Hand Person – The Strategic Advisor .................................................. 24

**Gate 8** – The Publicist / Marketer .................................................. 26

**Gate 9** - The Immersed .................................................. 28

**Gate 10** – The Individual/Empowerer .................................................. 30

**Gate 11** – The Idea Seeker .................................................. 32

**Gate 12** – The Poet / Author .................................................. 34

**Gate 13** - The Listener/Confident .................................................. 36

**Gate 14** – The Resourceful Creative .................................................. 38

**Gate 15** – The Nature Lover/Extremist .................................................. 40

**Gate 16** – The Talent – Master Experimenter
AKA Sprezzatura .................................................. 42

**Gate 17** – The Strategist / The Farsighted Pathfinder
.................................................. 44

**Gate 18** – The Critic .................................................. 46

**Gate 19** – The Thoughtful Host .................................................. 48

**Gate 20** – The Collaborator .................................................. 50

**Gate 21** – The Expert Resource Coordinator .................................................. 52

**Gate 22** - The Grace Giver .................................................. 54

**Gate 23** - The Alchemist .................................................. 56

**Gate 24** - The Explainer .................................................. 58

**Gate 25** - The Space Holder .................................................. 60

# TABLE OF CONTENTS

**Gate 26** – The Efficient Sales Person .................................... 62

**Gate 27** – The Protective Caregiver .................................... 64

**Gate 28** – The Risk Taker .................................... 66

**Gate 29** – The Tenacious Persistent .................................... 68

**Gate 30** – The Intense .................................... 70

**Gate 31** – The Reluctant Leader .................................... 72

**Gate 32** – The Successful Conservative .................................... 74

**Gate 33** – The Elder / Old Soul .................................... 76

**Gate 34** – The Empowered Individual .................................... 78

**Gate 35** – The Adventure Seeker .................................... 80

**Gate 36** – The Compassionate Depth Holder .................................... 82

**Gate 37** – The Community Maestro .................................... 84

**Gate 38** – The Purposeful Effortless Warrior .................................... 86

**Gate 39** – The Provocateur – The Provocative Artist .................................... 88

**Gate 40** – The Generous Provider .................................... 90

**Gate 41** – The Experiencer .................................... 92

**Gate 42** – The Finisher .................................... 94

**Gate 43** – The Insightful Genius .................................... 96

**Gate 44** – The Talent Scout .................................... 98

**Gate 45** – The Material Wielder .................................... 100

**Gate 46** – The Determined .................................... 102

**Gate 47** – The Aha Moment Stimulus .................................... 104

**Gate 48** – The Sage / The Well of Wisdom .................................... 106

**Gate 49** – The Revolution Leader .................................... 108

**Gate 50** – The Caring Parent .................................... 110

**Gate 51** – The Shocker/Early Adopter/Trend Setter .................................... 112

# TABLE OF CONTENTS

**Gate 52** – The Buddha ........................................ 114

**Gate 53** – The Starter ........................................ 116

**Gate 54** – The Ambitious Prosperity Seeker ........................ 118

**Gate 55** – The Spirited Artist ........................................ 120

**Gate 56** – The Wandering Story Teller ........................ 122

**Gate 57** – The Intuitive ........................................ 124

**Gate 58** – The Delightful Spirit ........................................ 126

**Gate 59** – The intimate Creative ........................................ 128

**Gate 60** – The Resourceful Optimist ........................ 130

**Gate 61** – The Truth Seeker ........................................ 132

**Gate 62** – The Sense Maker / The Abstract
Communicator ........................................ 134

**Gate 63** – The Inquisitor ........................................ 136

**Gate 64** – The Dreamer ........................................ 138

**Gate Summaries** ........................................ 140

**About the Author** ........................................ 141

**Resources & Additional Support** ........................ 143

# How To Use This Book

Hello & Welcome, Human Design Enthusiast!

I am delighted you are here delving deeper into the human design gates. The Human Design Gate Strengths book is my synthesis of how the gates are present in the wild. The intention of this book is to provide you with a reference guide for yourself and use it with clients when it comes to the human design gates.

The synthesis within the pages of this book, while simple, is not simplistic. The creation of this book was three years in the making. The information provided within the pages of this book is not a substitute for gaining mastery and depth around the gates. When I teach gates in my HD Wild Human Design Certification, I spend six months teaching the 64 gates in the chart. This book intends to support those who read, reference, and leverage it to find more alignment with the strengths in the human design chart.

My hope and expectation are that you use this for yourself to anchor into the gate strengths within your chart. The contents of this book will help you build a life and business you love at the intersection of your design, desires, and lifestyle. I hope you leverage this with your human design curious clients as a reference tool to come back to again and again when coaching, guiding, strategizing, and consulting clients.

I have synthesized and distilled down the most essential parts of each gate and included two pages for each gate. The first page describes the gate, themes of the high and low expression, the voice, and how that gate's energy supports others.

The second page includes questions that you can use with yourself or with your clients to find congruence with that gate. You will also find information on which center the gate is located in, its astrological sign, and its element.

Finally, I've included laser-focused themes for each gate's reactive, repressed, and victim mode presentations. I opted to include these presentations as a laser-focused way to find incongruence with the gate's energy for yourself or when working with clients.

I hope that this book finds a home on your desk where it is well-loved and leveraged regularly.

Thank you for stepping on the journey to get back to the nature of who you are before the world told you who you should be. Your commitment to leaning in and doing the deconditioning work for yourself and with others creates a ripple effect in the world.

With your design in mind,

Jamie

# How To Use This Book

Below you will find the breakdown of how the reference guide can be used and the breakdown of the information provided for each gate.

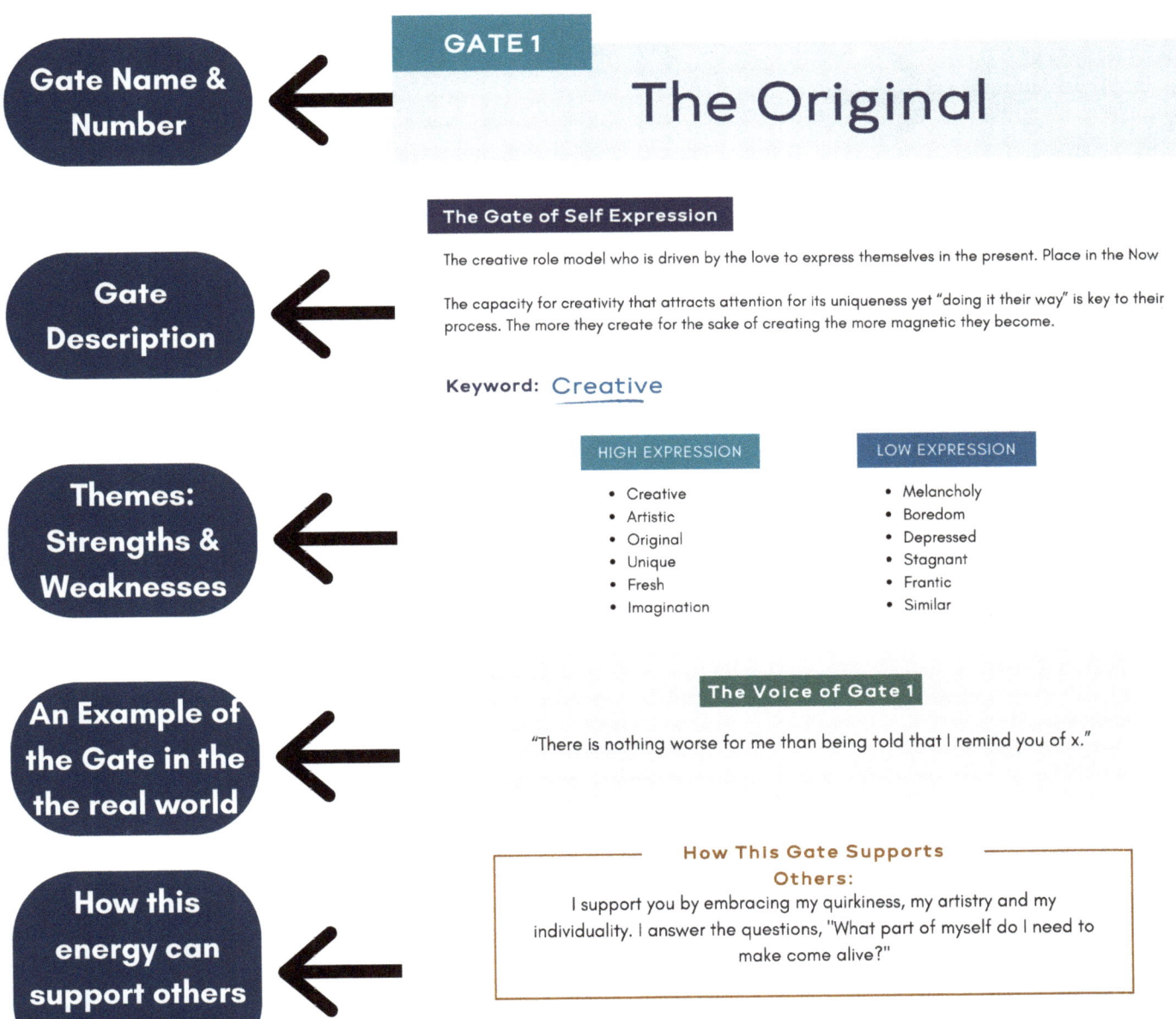

**Gate Name & Number**

**GATE 1**

## The Original

**Gate Description**

### The Gate of Self Expression

The creative role model who is driven by the love to express themselves in the present. Place in the Now

The capacity for creativity that attracts attention for its uniqueness yet "doing it their way" is key to their process. The more they create for the sake of creating the more magnetic they become.

**Keyword:** Creative

**Themes: Strengths & Weaknesses**

| HIGH EXPRESSION | LOW EXPRESSION |
|---|---|
| • Creative | • Melancholy |
| • Artistic | • Boredom |
| • Original | • Depressed |
| • Unique | • Stagnant |
| • Fresh | • Frantic |
| • Imagination | • Similar |

**An Example of the Gate in the the real world**

### The Voice of Gate 1

"There is nothing worse for me than being told that I remind you of x."

**How this energy can support others in life & biz**

### How This Gate Supports Others:
I support you by embracing my quirkiness, my artistry and my individuality. I answer the questions, "What part of myself do I need to make come alive?"

01

*jamielpalmer.com*

# How To Use This Book

Below you will find the breakdown of how the reference guide can be used and the breakdown of the information provided for each gate.

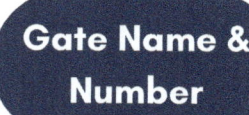

**Gate Name & Number**

GATE 1

## The Original

**Questions & prompts for alignement**

### Questions to Ask

- What is your relationship with self like?
- Do you feel free to express yourself and be an unique individual?
- What do you need to let go of to truly be yourself?
- How does it feel when someone tells you..."you remind me of x?"
- Where have you compromised or settled for fitting in?
- Are you feeling pressured to confirm to what society/culture thinks you should do?
- How could you better express your unique self?
- How do you express yourself ascetically in your clothing, style etc?
- Where do you feel safe to express yourself?
- What is your relationship like with self-love?
- Do you see yourself as creative? How do you own your creativity?
- Do you feel pressured to fulfill your purpose? How do you handle that?
- Do you have meaning in your life?
- Where do you feel frantic and why?
- How are you tending to yourself and your uniqueness?
- How do you express yourself?

**Gate Location Sign & Element Low Expression Presentations**

Gate of Self Expression

| Center | Identity | Repressive | Depressive |
|---|---|---|---|
| Astro Sign | Scorpio | Reactive | Frenetic |
| Element | Water | Victim Pattern | Numbness |

*jamielpalmer.com*                    02

# Gate Strengths Workshop

Visit hdgatestrengths.com or scan the QR code below to gain access to the 2 hours Human Design Gate Strengths workshop which is included with the purchase of this book along with additional resources.

# The Original

## The Gate of Self Expression

The creative role model who is driven by the love to express themselves in the present. Place in the Nov The capacity for creativity that attracts attention for its uniqueness yet "doing it their way" is key to the process. The more they create for the sake of creating the more magnetic they become. These are people above all else strive to be differentiated in all aspects of live including their appearance and clothing.

**Keyword:** _Creative_

| HIGH EXPRESSION | LOW EXPRESSION |
|---|---|
| • Creative | • Melancholy |
| • Artistic | • Boredom |
| • Original | • Depressed |
| • Unique | • Stagnant |
| • Fresh | • Frantic |
| • Imagination | • Similar |

## The Voice of Gate 1

"There is nothing worse for me than being told that I remind you of x."

## How This Gate Supports Others:

I support you by embracing my quirkiness, my artistry and my individuality. I answer the questions, "What part of myself do I need to make come alive?"

# The Original

## Questions to Ask

- What is your relationship with self like?
- Do you feel free to express yourself and be an unique individual?
- What do you need to let go of to truly be yourself?
- How does it feel when someone tells you..."you remind me of x?"
- Where have you compromised or settled for fitting in?
- Are you feeling pressured to conform to what society/culture thinks you should do?
- How could you better express your unique self?
- How do you express yourself aesthetically in your clothing, style etc?
- Where do you feel safe to express yourself?
- What is your relationship like with self-love?
- Do you see yourself as creative? How do you own your creativity?
- Do you feel pressured to fulfill your purpose? How do you handle that?
- Do you have meaning in your life?
- Where do you feel frantic and why?
- How are you tending to yourself and your uniqueness?
- How do you express yourself?

## Gate of Self Expression

| Center | Identity | Repressive | Depressive |
|---|---|---|---|
| Astro Sign | Scorpio | Reactive | Frenetic |
| Element | Water | Victim Pattern | Numbness |

# The Visionary

## The Gate of Direction

The Director who is driven by direction & vision by deciding what to do with what has been received. – The Direction or Driver. The innate ability to discern where someone or something needs to go - the acorn who knows it will become the oak tree. This energy needs to trust the vision it has and leap with faith that the resources will appear. Let go of rushing and being further along. Accept where they are and move forward with trust that their vision will come to fruition.

**Keyword:** Guidance

| HIGH EXPRESSION | LOW EXPRESSION |
|---|---|
| • Visionary | • Compromising for Others |
| • Direction | • Spending Carelessly |
| • Self-Worth | • Burnout |
| • Faith | • Refusing Support |
| • Authenticity | • Managing Resources |
| • Trust | • Trying to follow a formula |
| • Spender | |
| • Unique Path | |

## The Voice of Gate 2

"I really believe she should be doing x. I can see this and this in here and she is simply going in the wrong direction."

### How This Gate Supports Others:

I support you by understanding which direction is optimal for you. I answer the question, "what is the correct direction for me"?

# The Visionary

## Questions to Ask

- What is your relationship like with getting support?
- Do you actually ask for help with your needs?
- Do you have trust and faith that the universe has your back and your intentions will manifest?
- What is your relationship like with money?
- Are you open to receiving abundance? Do you have faith and trust in your ability to receive?
- Do you have doubts and anxiousness about your ability to receive? Do you worry that you will not receive?
- Do you trust your higher knowing?
- Do you honor the highest expression of yourself?
- What happens when you feel lost or disoriented?
- Do you abandon ship or reorient?

### Gate of Higher Knowledge

| Center | Identity | Repressive | Lost |
|---|---|---|---|
| Astro Sign | Taurus | Reactive | Regimented |
| Element | Earth | Victim Pattern | External circumstances |

# The Innovator

## The Gate of Ordering – The Format Energy of On/Off Pulse

The format energy that drives the (often melancholic) energy of bringing order out of chaos by accepting the limitations of the current structure- the process of innovation (that may or may not last) – frustration over the rigidity that exists on the material plane, waiting for the right timing (gate 60)

## Keyword: Innovation

| HIGH EXPRESSION | LOW EXPRESSION |
| --- | --- |
| • Newness | • Obstruction |
| • Learning | • Difficulty Starting |
| • Weird | • Rushing |
| • Innocence | • Meticulous |
| • Transformation | • Obsessive |
| • Change Agent | • Resistant to change |

## The Voice of Gate 3

"I'm so overwhelmed by _____ I wish I could create something new."

## How This Gate Supports Others:

Gate 3 – I support you with my tenacity, structure, patience, and inventiveness. I answer the question, "How can I be more disciplined so that I can find the limitations of this structure to innovate? What will have a lasting impact in the world?

# The Innovator

## Questions to Ask

- How can you honor the timing of your life?
- What does waiting for the right timing in your life feel like?
- When has patience paid off?
- How can you reckon with the near constant pressure in your life? When do you need to take time to explore?
- Are you ready to share your idea?
- What needs to be in place for you to feel ready to share your ideas? Where are you feeling/experiencing pressure in your life?
- Are you trying to control the chaos in your life? Or Allow it?
- Where do you feel chaos and confusion?
- What do you feel under pressure to share?
- Where do you feel called to innovate?
- How are you dancing with confusion in your life?

## Gate of Ordering

| Center | Sacral | Repressive | Anal |
|---|---|---|---|
| Astro Sign | Aries & Taurus | Reactive | Distorted |
| Element | Fire - Earth | Victim Pattern | Chaotic mind |

# The Solution Provider

## The Gate of Formulization

A reaction or response to a question, statement, or situation – may or may not be the correct answer – often future based. These are people who will always have an answer to any question that is asked and are under near constant mental pressure to produce that answer even if it is incorrect/untested/yet to be proven true.

**Keyword:** Answers

### HIGH EXPRESSION

- Problem Solver
- Possibilities
- Knowledge
- Potential
- Understanding

### LOW EXPRESSION

- Superstitious
- Suspicious
- Judgement
- Disaster
- Skeptical
- Anxiety
- Nit-Picky
- Intolerant

## The Voice of Gate 4

"I know the answer to that. This is what we should do."

"I should be less suspicious of x but _____."

## How This Gate Supports Others:

I support you with my ability to always have an answer (even though it may not always be correct.) I answer questions, "Ask me anything. I have an answer."

# The Solution Provider

## Questions to Ask

- What is the potential here?
- How can you embrace the possibilities of your ideas?
- How can you substantiate your ideas through facts?
- Are you allowing your doubts and anxiety to drive your decisions?
- Are you doubting your knowing and answers?
- Are you stuck in indecision because you are trying to search for answers?
- Are you feeling pressure that life may be in chaos because you can't seem to find the answer?
- Are you using the pressure you feel to provide answers for others? Or are you using it on yourself and it is keeping you in a holding pattern?
- Which of your many answers do you actually pursue?
- Are you seeking answers just to get rid of your doubts?
- Are you honoring the timing of these new possibilities?
- Which possibilities, potentials, and answers are stimulating to you right now?
- Do these possibilities/answers bring you pleasure?
- Which of your ideas have potential and need you to nurture them?
- Are you overtly relying on a formula too much?

## Gate of Formulization

| Center | Ajna | Repressive | Apathetic |
|---|---|---|---|
| Astro Sign | Leo | Reactive | Nit-picking |
| Element | Fire | Victim Pattern | Need for answers |

# The Consistent Dependable

## The Gate of Fixed Rhythms

People who have an inherent need to be consistent and routine in all areas of life. Routine provides security and health that drives energy to show up consistently and in routine through patters - frustratic over inconsistency - This is the gate of being able to persevere and have fixed patterns in life. If this gate is present you will need a consistent digestive pattern.

**Keyword:** Routine / Patience

| HIGH EXPRESSION | LOW EXPRESSION |
|---|---|
| • Consistency | • Pushy |
| • Empowerment | • Nit-Picky |
| • Routine | • Impatient |
| • Stability | • Overwhelmed |
| • Ritual | • Demanding |
| • Rhythm | |

## The Voice of Gate 5

"I'm so frustrated with the way x shows up. They are never consistent and it drives me crazy."

" I have to follow a consistent routine otherwise I am off kilter."

"I should make it mandatory for everyone to follow this routine at work because it is the best and works for me."

## How This Gate Supports Others:

I support you by showing up in a dependable, consistent, and habitual manner. I can be relied on to be routine, consistent. I answer the question, "What can we systematize, productize, make routine?"

# The Consistent Dependable

## Questions to Ask

- How can you honor your habits, routines and rituals as sacred?
- What habits are energy giving? What habits are energy taking?
- Where do you need to pause in order to become aware so that you can find your own rhythm?
- Are you honoring your rhythm or are you allowing others to interfere with what gives you energy?
- Are you holding onto routines that no longer fuel you?
- Where are you resisting creating routine in your life?
- What routine makes you feel connected to yourself?
- What environment supports your need for consistency?
- What habits do you need to let go of?
- What habits do you need to cultivate?
- What habits do you need to change?
- Are you projecting your need for habits onto other?
- How can you manage your need for consistency with others that do not have that same need?
- Are you being picky/pushy, impatient with others who are not routine?
- Is the environment you're in supportive of your rituals? What is your natural inclination or pattern?

## Gate of Fixed Rhythms

| Center | Sacral | Repressive | Pessimistic |
|---|---|---|---|
| Astro Sign | Sagittarius | Reactive | Pushy |
| Element | Fire | Victim Pattern | Impatience |

# The Big Family Or Multi-Preneur

## The Gate of Friction – Conflict

The Gate of Friction that drives the desire to be close to others but the fear of revealing yourself and being vulnerable. People who are designed to be discriminating both emotionally and sexually. This gat determines whether we are open or closed to intimacy. Nervousness over being open to others.

## Keyword: Intimacy

| HIGH EXPRESSION | LOW EXPRESSION |
|---|---|
| • Intimacy | • Defensive |
| • Boundaries | • Judgmental |
| • Breaking Down Walls | • Play Small |
| • Diplomatic | • Tackless |
| • Calm | • Helicoptering |
| | • Micro-Managing |

## The Voice of Gate 6

"I don't feel ready to try that yet because that requires me to really put myself out there."

### How This Gate Supports Others:

I support you in breaking down walls and barriers so that can you can become intimate and vulnerable with others. I answer the question, "What wall do you have up that you are ready to let go of so that you can cultivate more intimacy and vulnerability in your life?"

# The Big Family Or Multi-Preneur

## Questions to Ask

- How can you bring more peace to your relationships?
- What does sustainability, growth and serenity mean to you?
- Are you taking responsibility for your big, strong emotional energy?
- Are you making sure you are calm and grounded before responding?
- Are you creating intimacy from a place of serenity?
- Are you prioritizing the good of the community?
- What do you need to do to get grounded?
- Are you creating peace or war in your life?
- Do you fear you won't be heard?
- Where are you letting your defensiveness run the show?
- Are you allowing yourself to be emotionally vulnerable?
- Where do you find yourself nit-picking others?
- Where are you making decisions from a place of friction?
- Where are you being overly rigid?

## Gate of Friction

| Center | Solar Plexus | Repressive | Over-attentive |
|---|---|---|---|
| Astro Sign | Virgo | Reactive | Tactless |
| Element | Earth | Victim Pattern | Emotions |

# The Right Hand Person
## - The Strategic Advisor

## The Gate of the Role of Self

The gate of the role of self that is driven by progress forward and leadership. Direction Looking Forward The capacity for leadership yet it needs to be elected to lead so that it can gain influence/power. The gift for providing direction on where something needs to go in the future to better humanity. Breaking down the old in pursuit of something new. The logical expression of self.

## Keyword: Guidance

| HIGH EXPRESSION | LOW EXPRESSION |
|---|---|
| • Guidance | • Authoritarian |
| • Collaboration | • Ruler-eque |
| • Right Hand Person | • Jealous |
| • Service | • Dominant |
| • Future Orientation | • Trendy |

## The Voice of Gate 7

"I can see that x is going to become an issue in the future and we need to make a plan to address that."

"I rely on x because they have this innate ability to see into the future and see what might potentially be a problem."

"I should raise my hand be the leader."

## How This Gate Supports Others:

I support you by putting in a role where I am your right hand person. I answer the question, "What do I need to be mindful of up ahead? Where is there a fork in the road up ahead?"

# The Right Hand Person
## - The Strategic Advisor

## Questions to Ask

- Are you giving your power and patterns away and not being recognized for your leadership?
- What patterns are you recognizing that need to be articulated about the future of your community?
- Who are you influencing in a position of leadership or power?
- How are you directly influencing leadership?
- Who are you the support person, right hand (person) to?
- How are you cultivating relationships and leading the leaders?
- What is your role of leadership for the collective?
- What happens in your life when your primary role supports other leaders?
- Are you honoring the timing of your vision into the future?
- What are your gifts and strengths?
- Which leaders do you want to align with that have your values?
- Are you clear on your values? Which ones are non-negotiables?

## Gate of The Role of the Self

| Center | Identity | Repressive | Hidden |
|---|---|---|---|
| Astro Sign | Leo | Reactive | Dictatorial |
| Element | Fire | Victim Pattern | Jealousy |

# The Publicist / Marketer

## The Gate of Contribution – Holding Together -

The voice of I can. This is the creative ability to articulate, transform and promote. This gate needs to express it's own individual contribution to the collection and the individual contribution of others.

**Keyword:** Exquisiteness

### HIGH EXPRESSION

- Agent
- PR
- Expressive
- Contribution
- Promoter
- Stylish
- Exquisite

### LOW EXPRESSION

- Over giving
- Vulnerable
- Timing
- Purposelessness
- Self-sacrifice
- Fake
- Mundane
- Inauthentic

## The Voice of Gate 8

"I saw how _____ Jessica was and I know I can get her talents to come alive in this way."

### How This Gate Supports Others:

I support you by promoting, marketing, articulating what is unique. I answer the question, "How can I promote/marketing / get press for this? What makes this unique?"

# The Publicist / Marketer

## Questions to Ask

- Are you living the FULL expression of who you are or are you shrinking yourself down to fit in?
- Do you feel safe to express yourself?
- What is your relationship like with vulnerability?
- What has caused you to feel unsafe with sharing yourself and how can you let go of those experiences so that you can become?
- What is your relationship like with your authentic self?
- Do you feel free to express yourself?
- Are you embodying your unique expression or are you trying to do it?
- Where are you trying to be someone you are not?
- Where are others asking you to compromise with respect to your authentic self?
- What is the message you are trying to convey?

## Gate of Contribution

| Center | Throat | Repressive | Wooden |
|---|---|---|---|
| Astro Sign | Taurus & Gemini | Reactive | Artificial |
| Element | Earth – Air | Victim Pattern | Mundane |

# The Immersed

## The Gate of Energy for Detail – The Format Energy of Focus

The gate of determination that drives the ability to focus energy in a concentrated way to establish a pattern – frustration over channeling your energy on one focus. The ability to focus (or not) on and oscillate between the big picture and the details while knowing which are the essential details to concentrate on.

**Keyword:** Detail

### HIGH EXPRESSION

- Determination
- Focused
- Identifying
- Concentration
- Detail
- Staying Power
- Sticktuitiveness

### LOW EXPRESSION

- Restlessness
- Scattered
- Obsessive
- Squirrel Brain
- Fidgety
- FOMO

### The Voice of Gate 9

"I'm so frustrated and I can't seem to focus my energy on any one thing. It's like I have ADD."

"I should be able to get focused. What is wrong with me."

"I should stay focused on my goals but I fear I'm going to miss out if I don't say yes / do this thing"

### How This Gate Supports Others:

I support you in seeing the what is of value to focus on (or not). I answer the question, "What is worthy/deserving of my time/energy/effort to focus on?"

# The Immersed

## Questions to Ask

- Are you too focused on the details?
- Are you too focused on the big picture?
- Are you not focused at all?
- Is your focus in response to deepening your understanding?
- Is your focus in response to making sense/understanding something?
- How can you set your environment up for success to concentrate?
- Are you forcing yourself to focus?
- What are you forcing in your life?
- What do you need to let go of in order to regain focus?
- Do you have squirrel brain? If so when? Why? When do you notice that it emerges? What is the work you love to do and identify with?
- Are you forcing yourself to work when you have a squirrel brain?
- What does getting grounded and calm look like to you?

## Gate of Focus

| Center | Sacral | Repressive | Reluctant |
|---|---|---|---|
| Astro Sign | Sagittarius | Reactive | Diverted |
| Element | Fire | Victim Pattern | Details |

# The Individual/Empowerer

## The Gate of Behavior of Self

Gate 10 is driven by the love of one's self and individuality – Speaking & Living their own truth, fearlessly who Empowers others when in alignment – The Love of Self. In the low expression, this gate is concerne with what everyone else is doing and is wishing (& expecting) to be further along.

**Keyword:** Natural

| HIGH EXPRESSION | LOW EXPRESSION |
| --- | --- |
| • Self-Worth | • Self-Loathing |
| • Self Love | • Victim |
| • Courage | • Unworthiness |
| • Empowerment | • Settling |
| • Acceptance | • Blaming |
| • Equality | • Oversensitivity |

## The Voice of Gate 10

"I am an individual. No one is me and that is my superpower."

### How This Gate Supports Others:

I support you with my own courage to love and accept myself. I accept you exactly as you are. I answer the question, "What makes me unique?"

# The Individual/Empowerer

## Questions to Ask

- What do you love about yourself?
- How can you accept yourself for who you are and love yourself anyway?
- Are you criticizing others to make yourself feel better?
- Why do you believe you are not deserving of love?
- What self-loathing do you need to tend to and reckon with?
- What will make you feel worthy and deserving of love?
- Where do you need to move out of victim mode and take responsibility for your action? Where are holding onto blame/victimhood in your life?
- What do you need to let go of in order to accept and love yourself?
- How can you move from victimhood into empowerment?
- Where do you need to honor your individuality?
- What inner child wound do you have to contend with where you were shamed, criticized or nit-picked for being yourself?
- How can you claim back your power and individuality?
- What do you need to do to accept and love yourself?
- Where do you need to stop nit-picking others?

### Gate of Behavior of the Self

| Center | Identity | Repressive | Self-denying |
|---|---|---|---|
| Astro Sign | Sagittarius & Capricorn | Reactive | Narcissistic |
| Element | Fire - Earth | Victim Pattern | Self-obsession |

# The Idea Seeker

## Gate of Ideas – Peace

Creativity & inspiration around thoughts, direction and action not necessarily based in fact. The ability generate lots of ideas – most of which are for others. The anxiety of sharing and having your ideas stole and/or running out of ideas. The need to be discerning around which ideas to personally pursue.

**Keyword:** Ideation

| HIGH EXPRESSION | LOW EXPRESSION |
| --- | --- |
| • Ideas | • Gloom |
| • Illusion | • Lack |
| • Peace | • Block |
| • Reciprocity | • Hopelessness |
| • Steward for Ideas | • Force Ideas |
| • Attunement | • Empty |
| | • Anxiety over idea sharing |

## The Voice of Gate 11

"I have so many ideas and I can't decide which one I want to do. I could do this or this or this or this. I want to do them all."

### How this Gate Supports Others:

I support you in coming up with ideas - I answer the question, - "I don't know what to do next/pursue?

# The Idea Seeker

## Questions to Ask

- How are you stewarding your ideas and possibilities?
- What do you do when you face boredom? How do you handle it?
- Do you actually value your ideas?
- Do you believe more ideas will come?
- Are you hoarding your ideas?
- How can you be certain that now is the right time to share your ideas?
- Do you trust in the timing of your life?
- Are you forcing, pressured, or rushing your ideas?
- Do you feel valued by the people you are sharing your ideas with?
- How are you seeking, searching and cultivating new ideas?
- Do you feel at peace with the fact that you are not here to force ideas into the world? Which ideas are you selectively choosing for yourself?
- Are your ideas valued by others?
- What can you do to be better attuned to the timing of your life?

### Gate of Ideas

| Center | Ajna | Repressive | Fantasizing |
|---|---|---|---|
| Astro Sign | Sagittarius | Reactive | Deluded |
| Element | Fire | Victim Pattern | Beliefs |

# The Poet / Author

## The Gate of Social Caution

The Voice of I try. This is the ability to pull a story together and articulate the emotions of a situation or experience – these words move to me tears. I can feel the emotion of this story. The written or verbal expression of a story – the use of metaphor to express the peaks & valleys (emotions) of the human experience. This energy does not operate on demand. It operates on a creative urge when in the mood.

**Keyword:** Purity

| HIGH EXPRESSION | LOW EXPRESSION |
| --- | --- |
| • Creative Being | • Procrastination |
| • Auditory | • Stuck |
| • Powerful | • Restless |
| • Articulate | • Retreat |
| • Expressive transformative | • Moody |
| • Timing | • Forcing |
| • Wordsmith | • Stressed |
| • Discerning | |
| • Aloneness | |

## The Voice of Gate 12

"I tried my best to understand where they are coming for"

### How this Gate Supports Others:

Gate 12 – I support you with my power to change the way you understand the world around through my transformative words and timing. I answer the question, "What perception do I have that may need to be changed?"

# The Poet / Author

## Questions to Ask

- How are you using your words to spark transformation?
- Are you hesitant to share?
- Are you paralyzed by caution and therefore don't share even when you know the time is correct?
- Are you actually articulating your self-expression and creativity with the world?
- Are you honoring your moods?
- Are you feeling shy or bold?
- Are you spending time processing?
- What are you doing to connect to your creative power to express and give voice to words?
- Are you giving yourself time alone in order to process your insights to turn it into knowing?
- What is your relationship like with the pressure you experience?
- How do you work with the bigness of your expression and potential?
- What do your insights transform?
- Are you stepping into and owning your power?

## Gate of Caution

| Center | Throat | Repressive | Elitist |
|---|---|---|---|
| Astro Sign | Gemini | Reactive | Malicious |
| Element | Air | Victim Pattern | Need for perfection |

# The Listener/Confident

## The Gate of the Listener

Driven by listening to the stories of others and hearing secrets/reading between the lines of what is actually be said. – Direction Looking Back. This is the energy of attracting and sharing the experiences others as wisdom/lessons learned. Reading between the lines of what is being said to make sense of the past and extract the lesson so that a new cycle can begin from an elevated state. The collection of memories from the past is held in this gate. This is the Keeper of Secrets.

**Keyword:** **Reflection**

| HIGH EXPRESSION | LOW EXPRESSION |
|---|---|
| • Listening | • Stuck |
| • Historian | • Limiting Beliefs & Stories |
| • Keeping Secrets | • Grudges |
| • Reading Between the lines | • Gossip |
| • Discerning | • Pessimistic |
| • Empathy | • Narrowminded |
| • Generational Norms | • Generational Trauma |
| • Reframing Stories | |

## The Voice of Gate 13

"We should talk to x about company culture because they always seem to have a pulse of what is going on with everyone."

## How this Gate Supports Others:

I support you by understanding what is not being said and reading between the lines. I answer the question, "what needs to come to the surface? What's not being said?

# The Listener/Confident

## Questions to Ask

- What stories are you telling yourself that might be keeping you stuck?
- What is the subtext of this story you are being told?
- Are you giving yourself time to reflect?
- What limiting beliefs about the past may be keeping you stuck?
- What stories do you need to let go of?
- Are you hearing what is not being said?
- How are you using story to inspire others?
- What stories can you use to set a new direction for your life?
- Stories inspire possibilities. What stories can you share that provide possibility? What stories do you tell yourself?
- What story do you want to write or rewrite for your own life?
- When working with clients - is there something that needs to come to the surface? What emerges from this story?
- How can you use your listening to create more continuity?
- What vibrant threads emerge from all the stories that you have heard that provides learning for others?

## Gate of the Listener

| Center | Identity | Repressive | Permissive |
|---|---|---|---|
| Astro Sign | Aquarius | Reactive | Narrow-minded |
| Element | Air | Victim Pattern | Pessimistic mind |

# The Resourceful Creative

## The Gate of Power Skills

That drives energy for generating money and resources through doing creative work they love. Frustration over working endlessly and with no real sense of going anywhere. The need to do things in an individualistic manner and trust the resources will emerge.

**Keyword:** Abundance

### HIGH EXPRESSION

- Labor of love
- Money
- Managing Resources
- Entrepreneur
- Wealth
- Resourced
- Eccentric
- Passionate Work

### LOW EXPRESSION

- Fear
- Material Driven
- Enslaved
- Melancholy
- Over-worked
- Fear of Money & Responsibility

## The Voice of Gate 14

"I'm so frustrated I feel like I'm just spinning my wheels and not getting anywhere."

### How this Gate Supports Others:

I support you in discerning which skills (& the commitment needed) to bring a new creative project to life in the world. I answer the question, "What creative project is correct for me based on who I am? What skills / time commitment do I need to bring this to life?"

# The Resourceful Creative

## Questions to Ask

- Are you doing work that you love?
- Do you resist work that brings you joy?
- What work would you do if you didn't need the money?
- What resources do you have? What resources do you need?
- What is your relationship like with trust?
- Do you trust yourself with the resources you have?
- What is your relationship like with money?
- Do you trust that if you do things in your own way that the resources will be there for you?
- Are you doing work that feels aligned?
- How is your work transforming others?
- Are you clear on your purpose and direction?
- Are you doing it on your own terms, in your own way and marching to the beat of your own drum?

## Gate of Power Skills

| Center | Sacral | Repressive | Impotent |
|---|---|---|---|
| Astro Sign | Scorpio & Sagittarius | Reactive | Enslaved |
| Element | Water - Fire | Victim Pattern | Impotent mindset |

# The Nature Lover/Extremist

## The Gate of Extremes

Driven by a love of the rhythm of seasons and extremes of nature. The dichotomy that exists within nature. The Love of Humanity. This gate drives the energy of changing, adjusting and modifying rhythm based on what is happening in their lives. Thriving in diversity and remaining fluid rather than sticking to routine. Accepting without judgement the rhythms of others.

**Keyword:** Evolution / Timing

### HIGH EXPRESSION

- Accepting
- Embrace Diversity
- In the Flow
- Big Aura
- Good Memory
- Disrupt
- Fluidity
- Magnetic

### LOW EXPRESSION

- Shaming Extremes
- Forcing Consistency
- Balance
- Empty
- Purposeless
- Control

### The Voice of Gate 15

"Some days I wake up at 10 am and other days I am up at 5."

I know if I don't do x....so and so will do it for me."

"I should have showed up late so I could skip this small talk."

"I should have a routine but I just can't seem to stick with it."

### —— How this Gate Supports Others: ——

I support you with my ability to see the extremes in life and when it is time to shake things up. I answer the question, "Is it time for an evolution?"

# The Nature Lover/Extremist

## Questions to Ask

- Are you honoring your own rhythm?
- Are you free to follow your own flow or are you feeling you should have "daily habits?" Are you forcing yourself into someone else's rhythm?
- Are you sharing and judging yourself for not having a routine?
- Are you being conditioned by societal norms like routine?
- Are you committing to a routine / consistency and then not following through because you worry that you will not be successful if you're not consistent?
- What head trash about being consistent do you need to let go of?
- Are you forcing consistency on yourself because you SHOULD be consistent?
- Is your ego interfering in order to garner attention?
- Is there a proper balance in the extremes of your life?
- How can you build trust so that you can honor the rhythms of your own life?
- Where are you saying, "I told you so?" And how can you let go of that judgement?
- What narrow minded tendencies are you holding onto that are no longer serving you?

### Gate of Extremes

| Center | Identity | Repressive | Empty |
|---|---|---|---|
| Astro Sign | Gemini & Cancer | Reactive | Extremist |
| Element | Air – Water | Victim Pattern | Narrow mindedness |

# The Talent - Master Experimenter

## AKA Sprezzatura

## The Gate of Skills

The Voice of 'I think'. People with the ability to hone skills and gain mastery through repetition. People who have an enthusiasm to experiment in order to gain mastery. This is the voice of depth and mastery over time with a willingness to gain experience through repitition. This is the energy of the dancer becoming the dance which makes it look like the mastery is effortless.

**Keyword:** Loyalty

### HIGH EXPRESSION

- Enthusiasm
- Talent
- Mastery
- Experience
- Courageous
- Practice
- Repetition
- Focus
- Possibility
- Ability to make something look simple

### LOW EXPRESSION

- Moves Fast
- Unprepared
- Ego Enthusiasm
- Delusion

## The Voice of Gate 16

"Based on my experience, I think that this will work out the best because _____."

"I should probably do a bit more research before I jump in."

"I should probably take a bit more time to do x before I _____."

### — How this Gate Supports Others: —

I support you in getting into action to gain experience so that you can become an expert/master. I answer the question, "What is optimal for me to experiment with next?"

# The Talent - Master Experimenter

## AKA Sprezzatura

## Questions to Ask

- Do you see _____ as part of your identity?
- Where do you need to express and share your experiments in order to gain encouragement?
- Do you have a solid foundation to work from to experiment with?
- Have you done your homework before you jump into this next thing?
- Do you really know what you are getting into or are you leaping without looking? Do you trust your gut?
- Do you have balance between knowledge and experiment?
- Are you prepared to experiment?
- Are you allowing others to be the wet blanket of what you are enthusiastic about? Are you letting someone's lack of enthusiasm for your talents stop you from moving forward?
- Where is the energy for this experiment going to come from?
- What is something that you want to become?
- What work, skill, knowledge do you take for granted because it comes easy to you?

## Gate of Skills

| Center | Throat | Repressive | Gullible |
|---|---|---|---|
| Astro Sign | Gemini | Reactive | Self-deluded |
| Element | Air | Victim Pattern | Techniques |

# The Strategist / The Farsighted Pathfinder

## The Strategist / The Farsighted Pathfinder

People who have a gift for seeing potential possibilities in the future and form an opinion of what may happen. Perspective often based on fact and/or logic. The ability to see the many different paths to get to the goal from a 10,000 foot perspective.

**Keyword:** Future Potential / Integration

### HIGH EXPRESSION

- Possibilities
- Influential
- Exploration
- Of Service
- Strategic
- Long View
- Potential

### LOW EXPRESSION

- Being Challenged
- Exerting Opinion as Fact
- Dreamkiller
- Defiance
- Opposition
- Self-Critical

### The Voice of Gate 17

"In my opinion, it is best for us to do x first then do y because of the bigger picture goal/strategy we have in mind."

"I should let it go but _____ challenged me and I have to exert my opinion."

### How this Gate Supports Others:

I support you in seeing the many different paths/strategies to get to where you want to go. I answer the question, "What is the best way for me to get to x?"

# The Strategist /
# The Farsighted Pathfinder

## Questions to Ask

- How are you using your capacity to see possibilities in service of the greater good?
- Are you letting your possibilities hold you back from taking action because you feel overwhelmed?
- Are you judging others for not being able to see the bigger picture like you can?
- Are you holding space for another's opinion or are you exerting your opinion on others? How can you use your possibilities to expand?
- How can you resource yourself so you don't get fixated on a potential outcome?
- What can you do to manage your anxiety around potential future outcomes so you can get into action/expression/experimentation?
- Are you short cutting/bypassing your own success by looking for quick wins/shortcuts? Are you bypassing your own potential by going deep and looking for too many possibilities?
- Are you spending too much time learning and not enough time teaching?

## Gate of Opinions

| Center | Ajna | Repressive | Self-critical |
|---|---|---|---|
| Astro Sign | Aries | Reactive | Opinionated |
| Element | Fire | Victim Pattern | Opinions |

# The Critic

## The Gate of Correction

The ability to laser focus on what needs to be corrected – the ability to identify wounds, blocks, and barriers that keep people from living their life at its highest, most joyous expression. Our deepest conditioning comes from the parent who has this gate. This energy is not meant for use with individuals but for the collective.

**Keyword:** Integrity

| HIGH EXPRESSION | LOW EXPRESSION |
|---|---|
| • Re-alignment | • Picky |
| • Evolution | • Judgmental |
| • Continuous Improvement | • Superior |
| • Restore Joy | • Overly critical |
| • "Perfection" | • Fear authority |
| | • Perfectionism |
| | • Inferior |

## The Voice of Gate 18

"I know we just ate a five star restaurant but I really think they could have done a better job with x because _____.
"I should make this perfect before I put this out in the world."
"How can I make this better/perfect/the best?"

### ── How this Gate Supports Others: ──

I support you in spotting what needs to be corrected in order for you to live in alignment with your highest most joyous expression. I answer the question, "What needs to be reckoned with/ tended to / healed / fixed / corrected / improved upon in order to fulfill its potential?"

# The Critic

## Questions to Ask

- Is this vital or not?
- Is this correction going to bring you a sense of value?
- Are you invited to share your criticism to the individual?
- Will your judgement ultimately bring a sense of joy even if there is healing to do first? What judgement(s) do you need to release for your own inner critic?
- Are you feeling overly critical and therefore not sharing your insights with the world? Are you criticizing to right and to prove yourself? Or are you criticizing to heal, improve and for the betterment of the greater good?
- Are you mindful of the impact your criticism will make?
- Are you stuck because you are spending all your time perfecting?
- How can you work with the shame that you feel?
- Are you judging the collective instead of the individual?
- Are you mindful of the power of your conditioning critical words?

### Gate of Correction

| | | | |
|---|---|---|---|
| **Center** | Spleen | **Repressive** | Inferiority |
| **Astro Sign** | Libra | **Reactive** | Superiority |
| **Element** | Air | **Victim Pattern** | Judgements |

# The Thoughtful Host

## The Gate of Need - Approach

That drives the stress/pressure to be sensitive to one's own basic needs and the needs of the group. People who are under pressure to have their own material needs met but can self-sacrifice in the process or come across as needy to others. This gate harbors the gift of touch.

**Keyword: Awareness**

| HIGH EXPRESSION | LOW EXPRESSION |
|---|---|
| • Sensitivity | • Needy |
| • Awareness | • Isolated |
| • Keen to needs of the group | • Overly sensitive |
| • Gift of Touch | • Codependent |
| • Community Driven | • Self-sacrificing |

## The Voice of Gate 19

"I hate it when I have a empty refrigerator. I much prefer to have food stocked up just in case someone stops by."

### — How this Gate Supports Others: —

I support you with my ability to shine awareness on the needs of the group or individual. I answer the question, "How can I better support my people? What aspects of support are missing?"

# The Thoughtful Host

## Questions to Ask

- How do you work with your sensitivity?
- What is your relationship like with belonging?
- Are you prioritizing yourself first before the needs of others?
- What are your needs?
- What makes you feel resourced?
- How are you managing your own emotional needs first?
- Do you need to spend more time caring for yourself?
- What is your relationship like with the needs of those you care about?
- Do you feel clingy, isolated or co-dependent?
- Are you forcing intimacy?
- What boundaries do you have to make sure you care for yourself first?
- Are you martyring yourself for others?
- Are you losing your own identity in giving other people resources?
- What is your relationship like with vulnerability and intimacy?
- What is the emotional frequency around you? How does it make you feel?
- Are you interdependent or codependent?
- Do you have a partner you can rely on?

Gate of Wanting

| Center | Root | Repressive | Needy |
|---|---|---|---|
| Astro Sign | Aquarius | Reactive | Isolated |
| Element | Air | Victim Pattern | Over-sensitivity |

# The Collaborator

## Gate of Now – Contemplation – The voice of I am

The voice of I am. This is the voice of the person in the moment. In the present – collaboration over competition. People who are here to be enveloped in the moment. In order to be in the moment one is fully immersed, as soon as one says I am in the moment they are no longer in the moment.

**Keyword:** Metamorphosis / Breath

| HIGH EXPRESSION | LOW EXPRESSION |
|---|---|
| • Breath | • Superficial |
| • Contemplation | • Insecure |
| • Talent Scout | • Trying to DIY IT |
| • Collaboration | • Pressured Timing |
| • Aligned Timing | • Absent |
| • Brings People Together | • Hectic |

## The Voice of Gate 20

"I am honoring the timing of my life and I think now is the time to act."

### —How This Gate Supports Others:—

I support you best when I practice what I preach. I answer the question, "What makes me a unique individual? What am I talented at?

# The Collaborator

## Questions to Ask

- What makes you feel empowered?
- Where do you find yourself with hours passing by like seconds?
- Where do you need to allow more in your life instead of push?
- Are you allowing others to pressure you into action?
- How can you tend to your insecurities around empowering others?
- How are you dancing with the discomfort of others seeing you?
- Are you expressing your authentic self?
- What insecurity about "doing nothing" do you need to tend to?
- Who in your life has questioned you about what you are doing?
- What resources do you need to bring your project or creative endeavor to life?
- What stories do you need to reckon with in order to be empowered?
- Are you allowing yourself to be in the now or are you being pressured to be in the past or future?
- What can you do to ensure you are honoring the timing of your life?
- How can you let go of the pressure you feel to act from others and society?

## Gate of The Now

| Center | Throat | Repressive | Absent |
|---|---|---|---|
| Astro Sign | Gemini | Reactive | Hectic |
| Element | Air | Victim Pattern | Insecurity |

# The Expert Resource Coordinator

## The Gate of the Hunter/Huntress

These people thrive when in control of resources. People who are here to be materially independent wi
their resources – food, money, community, lifestyle. They thrive when they are have the freedom to be in
control and take ownership of that responsibility. This energy must first be responsible for themselves
before they can be responsible for other's resources.

**Keyword:** Directing

| HIGH EXPRESSION | LOW EXPRESSION |
|---|---|
| • Controls Resources | • Submission |
| • Freedom | • Overly Controlling |
| • Authority | • Passive Aggressive |
| • Caring | • Materialistic |
| • Trusting | • Lack |
| • Director | • Mindset |
| • Responsible | • Power Struggle |

## The Voice of Gate 21

"I'll do this myself because I know I can do this best."

### How This Gate Supports Others:

I support you with my ability to control resources (particularly money,
land, lifestyle) and be independent. I answer the question, "Where do I
need to take more control/let go of control? How can I budget so that I
can get x?"

# The Expert Resource Coordinator

## Questions to Ask

- Do you have the recognition and invitation before taking control?
- Are you respected in your community?
- What is your relationship like with responsibility?
- Have you been invited to take control?
- Is your control being interfered with?
- What self-control do you need to get better at?
- Are you focused on gaining experience?
- Where are you being overly controlling? In life? With others? With resources out of fear that you are not enough?
- What is your relationship like with your self-worth?
- What do you need to let go of in order to see the value you bring to the table?
- How do you self-regulate?
- What is your relationship like with control?
- Do you believe that you are worthy of support?
- What you doing to prioritize your own self-care?
- What is your relationship like with fear?
- What does it look like to release the need to control others and circumstances? Do you trust that you are supported?
- Do you over-compensate?
- Are you overly materialistic?
- What boundaries do you have in place that ensure you are prioritizing yourself?
- How are you serving the community?
- Where do you need to take responsibility?

## Gate of The Hunter/Huntress

| Center | Heart | Repressive | Submissive |
|--------|-------|------------|------------|
| Astro Sign | Aries | Reactive | Desperate Controlling |
| Element | Fire | Victim Pattern | Controlling Others |

# The Grace Giver

## The Gate of Openness – Grace

The need to be heard and the fear of not being heard. Fear of lack of growth. The gate of the left ear which only ever hears according to its emotional wave – only hears what it wants to hear. Nervousness over openness. These are people who need to honor their mood, above all else. They are powerful catalysts for transformation that spreads through others when they are open and in the mood conversely the opposite is also true. Please note this gates operates on a wave regardless of solar plexus definition

**Keyword:** Graciousness

| HIGH EXPRESSION | LOW EXPRESSION |
|---|---|
| • Grace | • Moody |
| • Honoring Oneself | • Too Self Focused |
| • Inner Beauty | • Diva |
| • Awareness | • Vapid |
| • Charming | • Vain |
| • Auditory | • Proper |
| | • Fear growth |

## The Voice of Gate 22

"I have so much to say but I'm afraid that no one is going to listen to me."

### How This Gate Supports Others:

I support you in tapping into your passions, desires and creativity. I answer the question, "What passion do I deeply desire to pursue that will transform the world?"

# The Grace Giver

## Questions to Ask

- Where are you settling or compromising for not pursuing your passions?
- What or Where are you denying yourself out of fear?
- How can you step into your passions and desires?
- What do you need to let go of in order to deepen your trust?
- What story are you telling yourself about why you cannot live a passion filled life? Are you obsessing over how you look?
- Are you honoring yourself and your inner beauty?
- What is your relationship like with your self-love?
- What is the unique contribution you are here to make in the world?
- Do you have the courage to follow your passions?
- Are you giving yourself permission to pursue your passions?
- Do you trust yourself?
- Who supports you? What evidence do you have that you are supported?
- Are you using your charm for good?
- Are you focused on your inner beauty?
- Are you overly focused on your material beauty?

## Gate of Openness

| Center | Solar Plexus | Repressive | Proper |
|---|---|---|---|
| Astro Sign | Pisces | Reactive | Inappropriate |
| Element | Water | Victim Pattern | Ungracious behavior |

# The Alchemist

## The Gate of Assimilation – The Voice of I Know

The Voice of I Know. This is the voice of knowing and certainty. I have this feeling, an insights that drops into consciousness through the minds eye. People whose insights must be invited to be shared, or they may be rejected and labeled.

**Keyword:** Simplicity

| HIGH EXPRESSION | LOW EXPRESSION |
|---|---|
| • Simplicity | • Uninvited Insights |
| • Digestible Information | • Fragmented |
| • Breaking Down | • Overly Complex |
| • Genius | • Judged |
| • Classy | • Rejected |
| | • "Freak" |

### The Voice of Gate 23

"I know this is going to sound weird, but I have this really strong insight that it is time to do x."

### How This Gate Supports Others:

I support you by providing individual insights, breakthroughs and inject new ways of thinking. I answer the question, "Which insight/innovation is worth bringing to life?"

# The Alchemist

## Questions to Ask

- What can you do to connect with your insights?
- How can you strengthen that connection?
- Do you actually trust the insights that pop into your head?
- What do you need to build your trust with your inner knowing?
- Are you making things more complicated than they need to be?
- Do you have enough depth?
- Are you keeping things simple?
- Do you actually trust what you know?
- How do you handle when you know something but you aren't sure how you know it? Are you with people who trust you and allow you to share your knowing?
- What wounds do you have to heal around being rejected for your insights?
- What evidence do you have for sharing your insights that has sparked transformation?
- How can you care for yourself so that you have more patience while you wait to share your insights with the world?
- Do you know something that isn't ready to be expressed in the world yet? How do you work with that energy?
- How do you connect with your knowing regularly?

## Gate of Assimilation

| Center | Throat | Repressive | Dumb |
|---|---|---|---|
| Astro Sign | Taurus | Reactive | Fragmented |
| Element | Earth | Victim Pattern | Complexity |

# The Explainer

## The Gate of Rationalization

This gates operates in the present moment going over thoughts (often obsessively), trying to rationalize explain or make sense of them. These are people who need time to contemplate the individual process and if something is actually original. These people hold onto mysteries & worries until they are resolved which often creates chaos, anxiety, & struggle in the mind.

**Keyword:** Rationalizing

### HIGH EXPRESSION

- Gratitude
- Sense Making of Past
- Investigative
- Inventive
- Rationalize
- Silence

### LOW EXPRESSION

- Settling
- Rationalize bad behavior
- Replaying Cycles
- Fixation
- Addictive
- Inexperience
- Naïve
- Ignorant
- Anxious
- No resolutions

## The Voice of Gate 24

"Let me explain. I did this because x and y and z. And because this makes sense if I go down this path then x, y, and z should happen."

### —How This Gate Supports Others:—

I support you in making sense of the past and rationalizing. I answer the question, "Do you have an explanation for _____?"

# The Explainer

## Questions to Ask

- What are you rationalizing or making excuses for in your life? What is repeating in your life?
- Where are you settling for less than you deserve?
- What are you grateful for?
- What lessons have you learned? And how can you use those experience to support others in growing?
- What do you need to surrender to or allow?
- What does it look like to allow yourself to live the life you deserve?
- What bad behavior in yourself (or others) are you rationalizing?
- What practices do you have to support you in silencing the mind?
- What ideas are rational and transformative?
- Are you hearing what is being said? Are you actually listening?
- Are you obsessing?
- Is your idea actually an original?
- Are you letting your mind drive the show?
- How can you put your mind to work for you?

## Gate of Rationalizing

| Center | Ajna | Repressive | Frozen |
|---|---|---|---|
| Astro Sign | Taurus | Reactive | Anxious |
| Element | Earth | Victim Pattern | Addictive tendencies |

# The Space Holder

## The Gate of the Spirit of Self

This gate drives the purity of spirit and self despite the circumstances that may emerge. This is the gate of Universal Love. This gate is the energy of deep compassion and understanding. These people love excitement and are initiated by life. This energy faces challenges on their journey that test and deepen their innocence & compassion – the goal here is to retain innocence, purity and understanding. People who need to spend time alone to integrate their experiences to create compassion. Optimally, life doesn't harden these people it brings them more innocence and childlike wonder.

**Keyword:** The Space Holder

### HIGH EXPRESSION

- Healers
- Wise
- Surrender
- Trust
- Selflessness
- Earth
- Nature
- Love of Spirit
- Healing
- Consciousness

### LOW EXPRESSION

- Jaded
- Restless
- Bored
- Selfish
- Cold
- Constricted Breathing
- Naïve
- Hateful
- Unworthy

### The Voice of Gate 25

"Even though x has happened it has brought me deep empathy for myself and for others."

### How This Gate Supports Others:

I support you in finding compassion, understanding and letting go. I answer the question, "What do I need to let go of in order to find solace/purpose/love/self-worth?"

# The Space Holder

## Questions to Ask

- Do you have trust in something bigger than yourself?
- Are you connected to your life's purpose?
- What is your relationship like with your experiences?
- Do you feel jaded and hardened? Or have you found more compassion? Do you trust in the seasons of life?
- What is your relationship like with nature?
- Do you have a connection to the earth?
- What does healing look like for you?
- What did you need to let go of?
- Do you need to spend time alone?
- How can you find more compassion for yourself?
- Do you feel worthy of love?
- Do you spread love?
- What is your relationship like with your purpose?
- Are you taking action from a place of ego from trusting in your purpose?
- Do you trust in the timing of your life?
- Do you honor the seasons of life?
- Do you take time to withdraw to regain your purity?

### Gate of The Spirit of the Self

| Center | Identity | Repressive | Ignorant |
|---|---|---|---|
| Astro Sign | Pisces & Aries | Reactive | Cold |
| Element | Water – Fire | Victim Pattern | Constricted breathing |

# The Efficient Sales Person

## The Gate of the Egoist

Drives the energy of efficiency and systems which allow for more play. People who are always looking f
the maximum reward for the minimal effort. People who can manipulate language to convince others.
The most reward for the least effort. The need to be mindful that they can deliver on their promises.

**Keyword:** Minimalist

| HIGH EXPRESSION | LOW EXPRESSION |
|---|---|
| • Efficiency | • Lying |
| • Marketing | • Manipulation |
| • Minimalist | • Egoism |
| • Artfulness | • Lack of Grit |
| • Truthful | • Selective Memory |
| • System Oriented | • Lack of Delivery |
| • Sales | • Low Self-Esteem |
| • Integrity | |

## The Voice of Gate 26

"I know we can do this in a more efficient way."

─── **How This Gate Supports Others:** ───

I support you with my ability to sell anything to anyone by making it
marketable. I answer the question, "How can I sell / market this with
more effectiveness? What is the hook?"

# The Efficient Sales Person

## Questions to Ask

- What is your relationship like with selling, marketing and efficiency?
- Do you feel pressured to work all the time?
- Are you in integrity with your promises/words?
- Do you deliver on what you say?
- What is your relationship like with your ego?
- Do you have a past lived experience, limiting belief or trauma that needs to be healed? Do you have the evidence that you can do what you are promising?
- What is your relationship like with self-worth?
- What is your relationship like with sales?
- Do you feel confident in your ability to sell?
- Are you mindful of your boundaries with work?
- What do you do to nurture yourself and replenish your value?
- Are you compromising your words because you are afraid that you can't afford not to?
- Do you spend time nurturing yourself so that you have more to give?
- Have you gained the necessary experience and forged yourself in the fire to exert your
- ego?

Gate of The Egoist

| Center | Heart | Repressive | Manipulative |
|---|---|---|---|
| Astro Sign | Sagittarius | Reactive | Boastful |
| Element | Fire | Victim Pattern | Egotism or Lack of grit |

# The Protective Caregiver

## The Gate of Caring

Drives the energy of nourishing and protecting oneself and others. Frustration over caring for everyone and anyone or no one, or lack of care for oneself. The mechanical energy of nourishment for people, places, and things. Guilt can be ever present in this energy. Radical self-care must come first for these people so that they can care for others.

**Keyword:** Compassionate

| HIGH EXPRESSION | LOW EXPRESSION |
|---|---|
| • Nourishment | • Guilt |
| • Nurturing | • Codependency |
| • Altruism | • No Boundaries |
| • Radical Self- Care | • Self- Sacrificing |
| • Gatherer | • Overly caring |
| • Compassion | |

## The Voice of Gate 27

"I am frustrated with myself because I have cared for everyone but myself."

## How This Gate Supports Others:

Gate 27 - I support you with how I nourish and prioritize myself first and set the example for self care. I answer the question, "What can I do to better nourish myself so that I can thrive? How Can I hold myself accountable to take better care of myself?"

# The Protective Caregiver

## Questions to Ask

- What is your relationship like with guilt?
- Do you take action because you feel guilty?
- How do you let go of the guilt that you feel?
- Would you make different choices if you didn't feel obligated? What responsibilities have you taken on that aren't yours? What is your relationship like with taking responsibility?
- What responsibilities do you need to let go of?
- What is your relationship like with caring for yourself?
- Do you overly care for others and forget to care for yourself?
- What are your values?
- Are you judgmental of other people's values?
- What reminders do you have in place to care for yourself first?
- What is your ideal self-care routine?
- How would your life change if your prioritized self-care first and others second? What impact could you make if you cared for yourself first?

## Gate of Caring

| Center | Sacral | Repressive | Self-sacrificing |
|---|---|---|---|
| Astro Sign | Taurus | Reactive | Self-centering |
| Element | Earth | Victim Pattern | Self-sacrifice |

# The Risk Taker

## The Gate of the Game Player - Preponderance of the Great

The Fear of Death, lack of purpose, and meaning. The gate of discerning what is worth fighting for, living for, and dying for. This energy has a resilence to it and does best when the odds are against it. This energy fears it will get to the end of it's life and think nothing had meaning or purpose.

**Keyword:**    **Resilient**

### HIGH EXPRESSION

- Persevere
- Resilience
- Grit
- Risk Taking
- Meaning
- Purpose
- Faces

### LOW EXPRESSION

- Fear
- Purposelessness
- Fear of Letting Go
- Defeated
- Victim Mentality
- Addiction
- Life is Unfair
- Hollow
- Fights for Everything or nothing
- Generational struggles

## The Voice of Gate 28

"What is my purpose in life? What is worth living for?"

### How This Gate Supports Others:

I support you in discerning what is worth fighting for / meaningful / taking a risk for in life. I answer the question, "What is my purpose in life? What risk is worth taking?"

# The Risk Taker

## Questions to Ask

- How can you forgive yourself for your past?
- What do you need to let go of so you can move forward?
- What have you learned from your challenges?
- How can you cultivate a sense of adventure in life?
- What do you fear?
- How can you use your "failures" as an experience to learn from?
- What do you need to tend to and reckon with so that you can learn to trust yourself again?
- What challenges have you faced that have been a blessing in disguise?
- Where do you like to be challenge?
- What about a challenge excites you?
- Where are you holding yourself back out of fear?
- Do you believe you are a victim in life? Do you feel like a failure? Why do you feel that way? What do you need to do to heal those wounds?
- Are you honoring and trusting your gut feeling?
- Do you trust your gut instinct/intuition?
- Are you sharing your struggles and your triumphs?
- What are the blessings / lessons from your challenges?
- Are you listening?
- Are you prepared to take a risk?
- Do you know what is worth risking?
- How can you develop a better relationship with your intuition? What can you do to be sure you are listening?
- What are your values?
- What makes life worth living?

## Gate of The Game Player

| Center | Spleen | Repressive | Hollow |
|---|---|---|---|
| Astro Sign | Scorpio | Reactive | Gambling |
| Element | Water | Victim Pattern | Fear of letting go |

# The Tenacious Persistent

## The Gate of Perseverance

Drives the energy to commit to an experience (often with the body) simply to discover the true potentia that lies within without the need to know where it will take them – the Fuel to Persevere. Frustration ove expectations of what the outcome will be. People who are here to say yes to life often because they don't want to miss out.

**Keyword:** Tenacity

### HIGH EXPRESSION

- Decisive
- Committed
- Persistence
- Cyclical
- Determined
- Devoted

### LOW EXPRESSION

- Over-Committed
- No Commitments
- Unreliable
- Controlling
- Burnt out
- Taken Advantage of

## The Voice of Gate 29

"I'm going to run a marathon just to see if I can."

### How This Gate Supports Others:

I support you with my determination and persistence because I show you what is possible in the world when you follow your drive. I answer the question, "Is this really possible? Am I really committed to doing?

# The Tenacious Persistent

## Questions to Ask

- What are you committed to that drives you?
- What are you saying yes to that leaves you feeling depleted and burnt out?
- What commitments did you say yes to but don't really want to follow through on? What is possible if you fully commit yourself?
- What do you need to let go of, obligations, commitments, things that you should have said no to in the first place?
- Are you saying yes to only things you know you have the drive to experience?
- What do you actually want to commit yourself to?
- Where do you feel driven to persist?
- Where do you succeed where others might fail?
- Where do you feel obligated to show up? How can you let that go?
- What are you committed to showing up for? How can you do more of that?
- What boundaries of your body do you want to test?
- What seems impossible but you sort of want to try?
- What do you need to give yourself a permission slip to go after?

## Gate of Saying Yes

| Center | Sacral | Repressive | Over-committing |
|---|---|---|---|
| Astro Sign | Leo & Virgo | Reactive | Unreliable |
| Element | Fire - Earth | Victim Pattern | Commitments or lack of |

# The Intense

## The Gate of Feelings – The Clinging Fire

The gate of desires that drives the desire to experience something new and the fear of feeling. Anxiousness about what may or may not happen. This gate is one of the most intense gates in the char and when present it amplifies in the rest of the chart. Nervousness over feelings and expectations. The fear the experience won't live up to the expectations. The feeling of the rug being pulled from below.

**Keyword:** Longing

### HIGH EXPRESSION

- Passion
- Desire
- Intensity
- Lightness
- Singular Passion ( Music, humanitarian, Science)
- Carefree
- Devoted
- Sensitivity
- Lightness

### LOW EXPRESSION

- Burnout
- Too muchness
- Intensity
- Indecisive
- Insatiable
- Serious
- Carelessness
- Conflict

## The Voice of Gate 30

*"I have been longing to do _____. I don't know why and I can't seem to explain it. I know if I do this it will bring me \*\*\*\*\*unrealistic expectations\*\*\*\*\*."*

### How This Gate Supports Others:

I support others by following my owns dreams and bringing them to fruition while balancing my intensity. I answer the question, "What am I yearning for, passionate about, or desire?"

# The Intense

## Questions to Ask

- What do you feel passionate about? What do you desire?
- Are you burnt out emotionally? Physically? Mentally?
- Are you moving too quickly because you are impatient?
- Is your intensity pushing people away from you because you are too much? Do you feel passionate about nothing?
- Is your intensity for _____ burning you out?
- How can you sustain your passion instead of letting it consume you?
- Are you pushing yourself too hard, too fast, too much?
- What are you feeling? What does emotional clarity feel like to you?
- How can you leverage your passion to drive your creativity?
- Are you overly worried about the outcome instead of enjoying the experience?
- Are you avoiding your passion out of fear that they will not come to fruition or that they are too unrealistic?
- Are you afraid of your own power/intensity?
- Are you being wise with your emotions?
- Are you afraid you are too much?
- How are you working with your anxiety?

## Gate of Recognition of Feelings

| Center | Solar Plexus | Repressive | Flippant |
|---|---|---|---|
| Astro Sign | Aquarius & Pisces | Reactive | Overserious |
| Element | Air – Water | Victim Pattern | Desires |

# The Reluctant Leader

## The Gate of Leading - Influence

The Voice of I lead. The sometimes reluctant leader who must always be invited and elected into leadership. Here to express the needs of the people they represent. This energy strengthens their leadership when they support their people in expanding. This gates uses words to influence others by speaking the truth of the group by listening first then influencing.

**Keyword:** Elected Leadership

### HIGH EXPRESSION

- The Face of the People
- Of service
- Listening
- Influence for Good
- Humble
- Powerful

### LOW EXPRESSION

- Know it all
- Needing Recognition
- Unworthy
- Bypass leadership
- Disrespectful
- Deferring
- Scornful
- Needing to be heard
- Arrogant

## The Voice of Gate 31

*"I was chatting with my people and we believe that x is best. So here I am speaking for the people."*

### How This Gate Supports Others:

I support you by being of service and listening to the needs of my community and using my influence when the time is correct. I answer the question, "how can I achieve my goals?"

# The Reluctant Leader

## Questions to Ask

- Are you embodying the message of the people that you are leading?
- Are you recognizing your fear of not being heard or seen and still taking action to lead your people?
- Are you being invited to lead or are you inviting yourself?
- Are you being recognized before leading?
- What does leading look like to you?
- Are you stepping into your role as a leader?
- Are you stepping into your role as the person who is elected into leadership and being of service to the people whom you represent?
- What do you want to be of service for?
- Are you taking time to listen to what your people need?
- Are you bypassing your role of leadership to someone else?
- What do you need to do to make sure you feel worthy of leading?
- Are you remaining humble in your leadership?
- Are you regularly spending time listening to the people who elected you to this role?
- What can you do to ensure you feel worthy when your time to lead comes? Is your fear or feeling of unworthiness holding you back for being a leader?

### Gate of Leading

| Center | Throat | Repressive | Deferring |
|---|---|---|---|
| Astro Sign | Leo | Reactive | Scornful |
| Element | Fire | Victim Pattern | Need to be heard |

# The Successful Conservative

## The Gate of Continuity – Duration

The Fear of Failure. The gate of discerning what is and is not of value or worth investing energy and resources into. People who are conservative by design. Here to ensure continuity from one generation to the next for the survival of the community, company, or people. People who fear failure and are often concerned with having enough monetary resources.

**Keyword:** Conservation

### HIGH EXPRESSION

- Conservative
- Successful
- Money
- Continuity
- Tenacity
- Endurement
- Discernment
- Remember
- Smell Failure
- Demand Respect

### LOW EXPRESSION

- Fear of Failure
- Indecision
- Too Conservative
- Impatience
- Avoidance
- Pushing
- Pushy
- Disjointed

## The Voice of Gate 32

"I just know that this is going to be a good investment. I can feel it."

### How This Gate Supports Others:

I support you with my ability to see the value of things and discern what next step/investment will support long term success. I answer the question, "What foundation do I need to have in place in order to achieve _____

# The Protective Caregiver

## Questions to Ask

- What do you need to do in order to bring your big idea into life?
- What do you need to prepare to cultivate your vision?
- Are you honoring the timing of your life or are you pushing?
- What is your relationship like with fear of failure?
- How can you cultivate more patience?
- Are you pushing instead of honoring your intuition?
- Are you too conservative? Too Prepared? Doing too much?
- Are you allowing your vision to unfold or are you pushing it to come to life? Are you stuck in indecision?
- Do you fear your ideas or dreams will be stolen from you?
- Are you worried about the timing of your life?
- Do you have a continuity plan in place?
- How are you working with fear instead of letting it drive your decisions?

## Gate of Continuity

| | | | |
|---|---|---|---|
| **Center** | Spleen | **Repressive** | Fundamentalist |
| **Astro Sign** | Libra | **Reactive** | Disjointed |
| **Element** | Air | **Victim Pattern** | Your idea of success |

# The Elder / Old Soul

## The Gate of Retreat/Privacy

The voice of I remember. This is the ability to recall, stats, facts, experiences and pull out the hidden lesson and wisdom that render the future generations better off so they can start from an elevated state. This energy gets wiser with time as it collects more experiences throughout life.

**Keyword:** Revelation

### HIGH EXPRESSION

- Reflection
- Nostalgia
- Stories
- Experience Gatherer
- Mindfulness
- Revelation
- Time Alone
- Memor
- Wisdom
- Hidden lessons
- Recall
- Storytelling

### LOW EXPRESSION

- Reserved
- Censored
- Stuck in the past
- Burnout
- Incorrect Timing
- Spread Negativity

## The Voice of Gate 33

"I remember when I was a kid and we would x....X taught us how.....and I can see how that will help better our future."

### How This Gate Supports Others:

I support you with my ability to listen to your story and find power in the pain that you have experienced. I answer the question, "All of this has happened. Can you help me make sense of it? What story do I need to hear? What lesson do I need to learn?"

# The Elder / Old Soul

## Questions to Ask

- How are you creating space in your day to day to reflect on your experiences? What stories are you telling yourself that may be limiting you?
- Are these stories / experiences that keep repeating?
- What stories do you have that spark a revelation in others?
- Are you honoring the timing of your story telling?
- Are you in the moment of the experience?
- Do you find yourself stuck with the stories you are telling yourself?
- Are you too reserved in your stories and therefore don't spark a transformation? How are you turning the pain of an experience into power or a revelation?
- What are the best ways for you to reflect?
- Are you jumping from thing to thing?
- Is glittery object syndrome causing you to repeat cycles?
- Are you finding time to listen?
- What stories do you tell that support people in finding a new direction? How can you build in space at the end of experiences to reflect?
- What does pausing to reflect and integrate the lesson look like to you? What is lesson or subtext of this story?

## Gate of Privacy

| Center | Throat | Repressive | Reserved |
|---|---|---|---|
| Astro Sign | Leo | Reactive | Censorious |
| Element | Fire | Victim Pattern | Your memories |

# The Empowered Individual

## The Gate of Power

The urge to display how different one is from others. This fuels the survival of the individual. That drives the pure power to empower. People who are independent, individual, and self-empowered – Frustration over not being able to use one's power in the present moment. If this is part of a channel it will be self-empowerment / individualization through intuition (gate 57), behavior (gate 10), activity (gate 20). The gate of being unavailable. This energy does not need to display its power all of the time.

**Keyword:** Power

### HIGH EXPRESSION

- Empowered
- Majestic
- Collaborator
- Self-Empowered
- Multi-tasker
- Powerful
- Timing
- Unavailable
- Convictions

### LOW EXPRESSION

- Bully
- Fearful
- Self-Absorbed
- Unconfident
- Unaware
- Self-detriment
- Forcing Power
- Struggle with relationship with power

### The Voice of Gate 34

*"I'm unavailable to do that now because I am working on x instead"*

### How This Gate Supports Others:

I support you when I own my own power and use it wisely. I answer the question, "where do I need to allow instead of push in my life?"

# The Empowered Individual

- How are you avoiding the power you have?
- Where do you feel weak?
- Where do you need to allow instead of push to create more alignment in your life?
- How can you find ease in your waiting?
- Do you have trust in the timing of your life?
- Why are you afraid of your power?
- What can you do to reckon with and tend to your fear of your power?
- What does a display of power look like to you?
- Are you being busy just to be busy?
- Are you pushing?
- Are you striving?
- Are you burning yourself out?
- Where are you forcing in your life and how can you let go of control?
- Are you being too present?
- Are you using your busyness as an excuse to avoid your power?
- What values are vital to you so that you know when to exert your power?
- Are you saying yes to work that doesn't use your vital powerful energy in an empowered way?

## Gate of Power

| Center | Sacral | Repressive | Self-effacing |
|---|---|---|---|
| Astro Sign | Sagittarius | Reactive | Bullish |
| Element | Fire | Victim Pattern | Your physicality |

# The Adventure Seeker

## The Gate of Change - Progress

The voice of I feel that drives the expression of experiences and lessons learned to the collective to spark evolution. The jack of all trades. The love of the experience and trying something new simply to understand what it feels like. Optimally, experiences don't repeat. If they do this means the lesson was not learned and the cycle repeats.

**Keyword:** Change

### HIGH EXPRESSION

- Challenging
- Exploration
- Story Telling
- Experienced
- Wisdom
- Capable
- Change
- New Experiences
- Adventure
- Boundlessness

### LOW EXPRESSION

- Jaded
- Restlessness
- Overconfident
- Unfulfilled
- Boredom
- Settling
- Goal Oriented
- Manic
- Repeating experiences

## The Voice of Gate 35

"I feel like trying something new because I'm bored."

### How This Gate Supports Others:

I support you by sharing my vast web of experiences in order for you to gain wisdom. I answer the question, " I have all this options. Which one do you think is optimal for me based on your experiences?"

# The Adventure Seeker

## Questions to Ask

- What can you take away from that experience?
- Are you letting boredom drive what you do next?
- What are you settling for?
- What did you learn from this experience that you can share?
- What is a story that has changed you which you can share?
- Are you sharing your stories?
- What is holding you back from sharing your experiences?
- Where is it time to make a change in your life?
- Are you saying no to experiences in order to avoid a challenge?
- What are you passionate /excited about?
- Where are you setting goals that are leading to disappointment?
- Write a list of experiences you want to have in your life.
- What can you do to support yourself in letting go of the outcome of an experience?
- Are you entering into this outcome free?
- Are you following your strategy and authority when you say yes (or no) to something new?
- Are your experiences repeating themselves? If so, what lesson do you need to learn?
- Do you need to take a moment to pause and reflect?

| Gate of Change | | | |
|---|---|---|---|
| **Center** | Throat | **Repressive** | Bored |
| **Astro Sign** | Gemini | **Reactive** | Manic |
| **Element** | Air | **Victim Pattern** | Need for change |

# The Compassionate Depth Holder

## The Gate of Crisis – The Darkening of the Light

The gate of crisis that drives the hunger to experience something new and the fear of emotional inadequacy. Nervousness over expectations. The ability to handle chaos and a dark night of the soul both personally & for others. Moving from a place of despair and chaos to hope and possibilities.

**Keyword: Subconscious**

### HIGH EXPRESSION

- Depth
- Openness
- Devotion
- Exploration
- Emotional Intelligence
- Clarity
- Rabbit Hole

### LOW EXPRESSION

- Chaos
- Crisis - Prone
- Dark Night Of the Soul
- Nervousness
- Vulnerability
- Inadequecy
- Creating Crisis
- Boredom
- Leaping without looking
- Expectations

## The Voice of Gate 36

*"I am struggling to tap into what I am feeling perhaps I should go try something new..."*

### How This Gate Supports Others:

I support you with my ability to handle emotional ups and downs by moving from pain to pleasure, inexperience to experience. I answer the question, "Could you share your experience with _____ with me?"

# The Compassionate Depth Holder

## Questions to Ask

- Where are you allowing your boredom to drive your life?
- Are you certain you have emotional clarity before you entered into _____?
- What do you do when you feel bored?
- What activities can you do when you feel bored to ensure you don't just try something new to relieve the pressure you feel?
- Do you honor the timing of your life?
- How have your experiences ended a pattern and created something new?
- What did you learn from your experience?
- Are you in a place of despair or of hope?
- What are you avoiding in an effort to prevent chaos?
- How do you handle crisis?
- What support system do you have in place?
- Do you know what emotional neutral feels like in your body?
- What lesson do you have to share from your dark night of the soul? How do you work with the chaos you experience in life?

## Gate of Crisis

| Center | Solar Plexus | Repressive | Nervousness |
|---|---|---|---|
| Astro Sign | Pisces | Reactive | Crisis-prone |
| Element | Water | Victim Pattern | Vulnerability |

# The Community Maestro

## The Gate of Friendship – The Family

The Gate of tradition that drives the fear to belong to a community and the fear that your needs won't be met. The worry that one will have to settle for tradition. The glue holding the family and community together. Nervousness over promises. The need to create a bargain that operates on a wave.

**Keyword:** Loyalty

### HIGH EXPRESSION

- Loyalty
- Bargains
- Inner Peace
- Community
- Food
- Harmony
- Nurturer
- Loyalty

### LOW EXPRESSION

- Weakness
- Overly Sentimental
- Cruel
- Gender Identity
- Fear Traditional
- Roles
- Manipulative
- People pleaser
- Looking outside oneself for peace

## The Voice of Gate 37

*"I'm worried that I made that deal and it doesn't seem like x is going to follow through on that."*

## How This Gate Supports Others:

I support you with my awareness of who is going to provide what is needed for you to be successful. I answer the question, "Who do I need next to better support me? Who can provide what is needed?"

# The Community Maestro

## Questions to Ask

- What habits, practices and routines do you need to cultivate so that you can have inner peace?
- How do you resource yourself?
- What does inner peace look like to you?
- What practices do you have that support you when you are out of alignment with harmony?
- What can you do to become more aware when you are at an emotional high or low?
- Do you recognize when you feel disharmony? Or does your wave explode?
- What values are important to you?
- Do you know who can support you?
- Do you know what resources you need?
- How do you work with your sensitivity vs against it?
- Do you see yourself as weak?
- Are you trying to control the world around in order to create peace?
- How do you handle chaos and disruption?
- What if you prioritize your own peace first? What would that look like?
- Are you holding on to stuff that disturbs your peace?
- What does sustainable inner peace mean to you?
- Have you articulated your frustration to others when they don't meet your expectations or do you just do it yourself?

## Gate of Friendship

| Center | Solar Plexus | Repressive | Over-sentimental |
|---|---|---|---|
| Astro Sign | Pisces | Reactive | Cruel |
| Element | Water | Victim Pattern | Gender identity |

# The Purposeful Effortless Warrior

## The Gate of the Fighter - Opposition

The energy that drives the stress and pressure to struggle in life and to know what is worth fighting for and living for. This energy stands for its independence even when the odds are against it to bring more purpose to life. Clarity around purpose, values and beliefs is key here to know what to fight for.

**Keyword:** Effortlessness

### HIGH EXPRESSION

- Effortlessness
- Warrior
- Resilience
- Visionary
- Honor
- Stubborn
- What's worth fighting for
- Meaning
- Perseverance
- Auditory
- Risk Taking

### LOW EXPRESSION

- Opposition
- Stubborn
- Woe is me
- Antagonizing
- Victim
- Defeatist
- Wrong Struggles
- Projection
- Deaf

## The Voice of Gate 38

*"I feel under tremendous pressure to find my purpose in life."*

### How This Gate Supports Others:

I support you with ability to craft a vision and stick with it. My stubbornness and resilience ensures you do not compromise your values, purpose or meaning in life. I answer the question, "What is my vision? Is it meaningful / original / worth fighting for?"

# The Purposeful Effortless Warrior

## Questions to Ask

- Do you know what is worth fighting for in life?
- Are you clear on your core values?
- Do you ever get swept into a fight when it is not your fight to fight?
- What is truly valuable in life to you?
- How are you using your experience/struggles/challenges in order to create a vision for the future?
- Are you bringing something meaningful into the world?
- How can you use your struggles to create meaning in the world?
- What is precious to you in this life?
- Are you honoring your intuition of when it is time to fight? Listen? Struggle? Challenge?
- Are you fighting someone else's fight?
- What is worthwhile and meaningful to you?
- What experiences do you have in life that could be truly valuable for others?
- What vision do you want to bring to the world?
- What brings you meaning and value in life?
- How are you using your struggles to provide understanding?
- Are you using your auditory powers?
- Are you tapping into your intuition and instincts to honor the timing of your life?
- When you are old, what will have brought meaning and value to this one precious life?

## Gate of The Fighter

| Center | Root | Repressive | Defeatist |
|---|---|---|---|
| Astro Sign | Capricorn | Reactive | Aggressive |
| Element | Earth | Victim Pattern | Belief you have to struggle |

# GATE 39

# The Provocateur -
# The Provocative Artist

## The Gate of Provocation

Drives the stress and pressure to find passion and evoke. The Gate of Deafness so that the muse survive This energy isn't always aware that it provokes. It is constantly seeking out others who resonates with it through provocation. This energy copes with stress by eating (or not). It is always seeking the perfect mood. The energy can be unaware which results in leaving a wake of drama behind it.

**Keyword:** Provocative

### HIGH EXPRESSION

- Provocation
- Dynamism
- Activist
- Consciousness
- Shifts others to Abundance
- Auditory
- Liberation

### LOW EXPRESSION

- Hoarding
- Eating Issues
- Triggering
- Provoking Drama
- Stress Eating
- Needy
- Deaf
- Trapped
- Moody
- Tense bodies

## The Voice of Gate 39

*"I love testing people's spirit just to see how they will react."*
*"I should do this even thought I'm not in the mood." (and because I showed up not in the mood I created drama for myself)*

### How This Gate Supports Others:

I support you with my ability to provoke your emotions and creativity to gain consciousness /clarity on a project. I answer the question, "I am experiencing a creative block. Can you help me unleash my creativity / passions / desires?"

# The Provocateur -
# The Provocative Artist

## Questions to Ask

- What will allow you to feel like you are enough? How do you know when you are enough?
- Do you have enough?
- How do you handle stress?
- Are you in your power to create?
- How can you take back your power?
- How are you working with your triggering nature?
- What are you doing to get the stress out of your body?
- What is your relationship like with sweets or food?
- How do you handle stress?
- Where in your body does it feel tight?
- Are you connected to your inner muse?
- Are you provoking just to provoke?
- Are you causing unnecessary drama in life?
- Are you honor your moods? Or are you leaving an emotional wake behind you?

## Gate of The Provocateur

| Center | Root | Repressive | Trapped |
|---|---|---|---|
| Astro Sign | Cancer | Reactive | Provocative |
| Element | Water | Victim Pattern | Your moods |

# The Generous Provider

## The Gate of Aloneness –

Driven to work hard but must balance that with times of rest. These are people who when they are restored, renewed and replenished have more inner and outer resources to give to the community. This is the gate of the breadwinner. In order to be in the high expression, this energy must establish clear boundaries, communicate them AND what it expects in return.

**Keyword:** Provider

### HIGH EXPRESSION

- Breadwinner
- Homebody
- Aloneness
- Hero
- Supporter
- Loves to Work
- Resolve
- Willpower
- Balance

### LOW EXPRESSION

- Too Much Peopling
- Fatigue
- Denial
- Lonely
- Digestive & Stomach Issues
- Workaholism
- Trying to save the day
- Not Caring For One Self

### The Voice of Gate 40

*"I love to work but I need to balance my work with time to rest."*

### How This Gate Supports Others:

I support you with my ability to connect, support and bring people together in community. I answer the question, "How can I do this with more sustainability / congruence / alignment?"

# The Generous Provider

## Questions to Ask

- Are you prioritizing your need for alone time?
- Are you martyring yourself in order to care for others?
- Do you feel alone? Do you doubt the value you bring to the table because you feel alone?
- Are you compromising your value for others?
- Do you value yourself? What is your relationship like with self worth?
- What do you need to let go of and reckon with in order to take responsibility for your self-care and your self-worth?
- Are you blaming or martyring yourself for others?
- Do you value yourself enough to take time alone in order to restore yourself first?
- Are you giving away your power when it comes to self-care?
- Where did you make a bargain, and fail to value yourself?
- What do you need to do in order to resource yourself first?
- What is your relationship like with guilt? Do you feel guilty for taking time alone in order to restore your own resources?
- Are you fatigued? What do you need to do to recharge?
- What work do you love?
- What bargains do you need to renegotiate in order to feel valued?

## Gate of Aloneness

| Center | Heart | Repressive | Acquiescent |
|---|---|---|---|
| Astro Sign | Virgo | Reactive | Contemptuous |
| Element | Earth | Victim Pattern | Fatigue |

# The Experiencer

## The Gate of Contraction – Decrease

Drives the stress or pressure to feel and try new experiences. People who have a near constant urge to experience new feelings and spend time fantasying about what could be. This energy has to be mindful about the expectations it places on experiences as it can often be left disappointed. This energy operates in the moment and only reflects on the experience after it is complete.

**Keyword:** Dreamer

### HIGH EXPRESSION

- Imagination
- Creativity
- Dreamer
- Vision
- Possibilities
- Limitless
- Anticipation
- Initiator

### LOW EXPRESSION

- Doomsday
- Fixation
- Worst-Case Scenarios
- Abdicating Creativity & Power
- Fear of Judgement
- Unrealistic
- Inaction
- hyperactivity
- Stuck Daydreaming
- Timing

## The Voice of Gate 41

*"I don't know why but I feel called to try this new activity just to see what the experience is like."*

### How This Gate Supports Others:

I support you with my limitless imagination and daydreams to generate new possibilities in the world . I answer the question, "What new opportunity / idea do you imagine with _____?"

# The Experiencer

## Questions to Ask

- Are you owning your creative power, expression and vision?
- Are you holding and sustaining your vision / creative power in spite of what others may say or think?
- Are you letting people tell you your dreams are unrealistic and therefore giving away your power?
- How are you regularly expressing your creative power?
- What feeling, desire or fantasy do you want to focus on experiencing?
- How are you letting go/managing your expectations, so you don't hit an emotional low? Are you focused on one desire?
- What do you need to do to tend to your fear of judgement?
- How can you honor your need to dream? What does honoring your dreams look like to you?
- Are you holding steadfast to your vision for the future?
- What is your relationship with your imagination?
- How can you embrace the possibilities to bring about transformation in your world?
- What are you fixating on?
- What worst case scenarios are you allowing to run your life?
- Where are you abdicating your power?
- Who is a dream killer in your life? How can you take your power back in your relationship with them?
- Are you projecting worst case scenarios onto others?
- Where are others projecting onto you and telling you you're unrealistic?

## Gate of Contraction

| Center | Root | Repressive | Dreamy |
|---|---|---|---|
| Astro Sign | Aquarius | Reactive | Hyperactive |
| Element | Air | Victim Pattern | Your dreams |

# The Finisher

## The Gate of Growth – The Format Energy of Finishing/Closing Cycles

Drives the energy of finishing the things that they begin - frustration over new beginnings and being stuck in cycles that seem to repeat endlessly. This energy is here to finish the cycle/experience, pause before entering into a new cycle to reflect on the lessons learned so that it can start the next cycle from an elevated state.

**Keyword:** Celebration

### HIGH EXPRESSION

- Finishing
- Growth
- Celebration
- Detachment
- Completing Cycles
- Increase
- People Person
- Experience

### LOW EXPRESSION

- Holding On
- Rushing
- Repeated Cycles
- Indecision
- Freeze
- Not Starting
- Self-judgement
- Quitting
- Depression

## The Voice of Gate 42

*"This is like groundhog day. I am so frustrating with doing the same thing over and over again and being stuck of this cycle but never bringing _____ to fruition."*

### How This Gate Supports Others:

I support you with my ability to finish. I answer the question, "What can you help me finish? What needs to be completed so that I can start something new?'

# The Finisher

## Questions to Ask

- Are you honoring your natural ability to finish things?
- What do you need to finish in order to make room for something new?
- Are cycles repeating in your life? If so what do you need to do in order to close them? Are you over committing yourself to projects because you know you can finish them but they aren't your projects to finish?
- What are you holding on to because it feels safe? What are you afraid to finish?
- How can you have compassion for yourself when it comes to starting?
- What are you frustrated over starting? Are you in a state of indecision?
- Do you value your ability to finish?
- How can you be less self-critical for your struggle to start something?
- Where are you stretched too thin?
- How can you reclaim your power with the projects you said yes to finish but aren't optimal (or yours) for you to finish?
- Do you have a backlog of projects to finish? If so, why?
- Are you frustrated about all the things you said yes to finishing?
- How can you build trust with your sacral response to finish? Do you trust it?
- What are you holding on to that keeps repeating that you need to let go of? Habits?Patterns? Activities?
- What can you do to be more compassionate with yourself? How can you ensure you only say yes to finish in alignment with your authority?
- Are you rushing/forcing finishing just so you can be done?
- What did you learn from finishing?
- Are you avoiding finishing because you know that means you will need to expand, grow or evolve?

### Gate of Growth

| Center | Sacral | Repressive | Grasping |
|---|---|---|---|
| Astro Sign | Aries | Reactive | Flaky |
| Element | Fire | Victim Pattern | Your expectations |

# The Insightful Genius

## The Gate of Insights - Breakthrough

The energy of drop-ins or out of the blue intuitive guidance and awareness that seemingly comes into consciousness from the mind's eye. This energy must be invited by the other so that the information is received. The fear of rejection. The gate of inner knowing which must be experienced for oneself.

**Keyword:** Breakthrough

### HIGH EXPRESSION

- The Muse
- Efficiency
- Epiphany
- Insight
- Breakthrough
- Transformational
- Brilliant

### LOW EXPRESSION

- Rejection
- Ignored
- Dismissed
- Inefficiency
- Deafness
- Worried
- Noisy
- Need to be Right
- Not trusting
- Lonely
- Melancholy
- Uninvited insights

## The Voice of Gate 43

*"I know this might seem strange or out of the blue but I just had this drop in (or message) come in and it is regarding your business. Do you mind if I share it with you?"*

### How This Gate Supports Others:

I support you in having an insight or a drop in that is "out of the blue" or unexpected. I answer the question, "What needs to be healed, reckoned with, or tended to in order for me to have a breakthrough?"

# The Insightful Genius

## Questions to Ask

- Are you honoring the timing in your life?
- What can you do to develop more trust with your inner knowing?
- What are you holding on to that needs to be released so you can better trust your own inner knowing.
- Are you honoring your need to spend time alone to hear your own inner thoughts?
- Do you trust that you will be able to express your inner knowing?
- How can you deepen your connection with your knowing?
- Do you have evidence of when your knowing was correct?
- Do you fear that you will be rejected for your insights?
- Are you being invited to share your knowledge?
- What do you need to heal with your fear of rejection?
- What story of rejection do you keep telling yourself?
- Do you know what the felt sense of recognition feels like in your body?
- Where has your inner knowing provided a breakthrough?
- Who do you trust that you can share your insights with?
- What do you need to let go of so that you can build trust with your inner knowing?

## Gate of Insight

| Center | Ajna | Repressive | Worried |
|---|---|---|---|
| Astro Sign | Scorpio | Reactive | Noisy |
| Element | Water | Victim Pattern | Needing to be right |

# The Talent Scout

## The Gate of Alertness – Coming Together

The gate for sensing (often via smell) the gifts, skills and potential of others. The instinctive knowing of someone else's capabilities. The fear the past is going to be repeated. The gate where past memories are stored which creates fear that failure will repeat.

**Keyword:** Hunch

### HIGH EXPRESSION

- Healing
- Teamwork
- Past Patterns
- High Aesthetic
- Symmetry
- Spot Talent
- Intuitive
- Entrepreneur
- Senses Gifts

### LOW EXPRESSION

- Distrustful
- Isolated
- Misjudging
- Fear of the Past Repeating
- Stuck
- Limiting Beliefs
- Cold

## The Voice of Gate 44

*"I'm afraid that because x happened in the past it is going to happen again."*

### How This Gate Supports Others:

I support you with my ability to spot talent and heal past patterns of mistakes. I answer the question, "Who has the skill to be in this role? What patterns need to be healed in order for me to break through my limiting beliefs?"

# The Talent Scout

## Questions to Ask

- What are you holding on to that needs to be released so you can better trust your own inner knowing.
- Are you honoring your need to spend time alone to hear your own inner thoughts?
- Do you trust that you will be able to express your inner knowing?
- How can you deepen your connection with your knowing?
- Do you have evidence of when your knowing was correct?
- Do you fear that you will be rejected for your insights?
- Are you being invited to share your knowledge?
- What do you need to heal with your fear of rejection?
- What story of rejection do you keep telling yourself?
- Do you know what the felt sense of recognition feels like in your body?
- Where has your inner knowing provided a breakthrough?
- Who do you trust that you can share your insights with?
- What do you need to let go of so that you can build trust with your inner knowing?
- What do you do when you notice a pattern repeating itself?
- How do you work with your fear instead of letting it define you?
- How can you better trust your intuition? Do you have evidence for when your intuition was correct?
- What intuitive insights do you have to share?
- Where do you smell something is off?
- What smells right?

## Gate of Alertness

| Center | Spleen | Repressive | Distrustful |
|---|---|---|---|
| Astro Sign | Scorpio | Reactive | Misjudging |
| Element | Water | Victim Pattern | Isolation |

# The Material Wielder

## The Gate of the Gatherer – Gathering Together

The entrepreneur or the expert – The Voice of I have. This is the language of I, me, mine. This energy speaks to the wants and the desires of the ego which educates the people. They are here to oversee and direct the resources – health, wealth, and efficiency of the community.

**Keyword:** Leadership

### HIGH EXPRESSION

- Leadership
- Generous CEO
- Sharing Resources
- Voice of the Community
- Synthesis
- Efficiency of Community
- Doesn't Get Hand Dirty

### LOW EXPRESSION

- Timid
- Arrogant
- Lack Mindset
- Self-Importance
- Show off
- Challenges
- Authority
- Show Off
- Overly Dominant

## The Voice of Gate 45

*"I am the one who is going to lead this"*

### How This Gate Supports Others:

I support you by better understanding how to manage and be more efficient with your resources . I answer the question, "How can we do this more efficiently?"

# The Material Wielder

- What is your relationship like with being a leader?
- Are you a selfish leader? Or a leader of the people?
- Do you own your voice?
- Are you afraid to lead?
- Do you shrink yourself for others?
- What do you need to tend to and reckon with in order to own your power, voice and leadership?
- Are you overcompensating?
- Are you pushing to hard to be put into leadership instead of being recognized and invited?
- Are you taking responsibility for gaining experience first before leading?
- Are you silencing your own voice and holding yourself back?
- How are you using your resources in pursuit of the greater good?
- What are you here to be a leader of?
- What is your leadership style?
- Do you trust that you will be asked to lead the right people at the right time?
- Do you fear that you will be passed over as a leader?
- Do you trust that timing of your life?
- What is your relationship like with abundance and success?
- Do you trust that abundance will show up for you?
- What do you need to let go of in order to trust your ability to lead?

Gate of Gatherer

| Center | Throat | Repressive | Timid |
|---|---|---|---|
| Astro Sign | Gemini | Reactive | Pompous |
| Element | Air | Victim Pattern | Poverty consciousness |

# The Determined

## The Gate of Determination

Driven by readiness & determination of entering into something simply for the experience of it often by testing the limits. The Love of the Body - caring for the temple. This is the energy of the athlete who wants to see what their body can endure simply for the experience of trying it. This is the love of the body & the magic of trusting ourselves in order to find the correct timing. People who fail where most succeed and succeed where most fail.

**Keyword:** Determination

### HIGH EXPRESSION

- Determined
- Driven
- Grounded
- Loving
- Delight
- Autumn
- Trusting Life & Body
- Body is a temple
- Embodied
- Serendipity
- Direction

### LOW EXPRESSION

- Overly Serious
- Frivolous
- Disregard for Body
- Obsessing over Body
- Misalignment Presents in Body
- Over Confident

## The Voice of Gate 46

*"My body is a temple and I treat it well even though I try to push the limits of what it can do simple to see how it feels."*

### How This Gate Supports Others:

I support you in embodiment and loving your body. I answer the question, "what do I need to do in order to nourish, care for, and be grounded in my body?"

# The Determined

## Questions to Ask

- What is your relationship like with your body?
- What practices do you have to nourish, care for and tend to your body?
- What do you love about your body? What do you hate?
- What do you do that brings you more energy?
- Your body will give you a sense of your well-being. How in alignment are you? What is your relationship like with your body image?
- What are you doing that brings you joy?
- Are you trying to force an outcome or look for good things in life?
- How are you being in the moment of an experience?
- What part of your body do you love the most and why? What part of your body do you love the least and why? What are you dedicated to that brings you joy?
- Are you being yourself?
- How can you better embody yourself?
- What brings you self-fulfillment?
- What are you resisting?
- Where do you need to lean in and say yes?
- What do you need to give yourself a permission slip for?

> ## Gate of The Determination of the Self

| Center | Identity | Repressive | Frigid |
|---|---|---|---|
| Astro Sign | Virgo & Libra | Reactive | Frivolous |
| Element | Earth - Air | Victim Pattern | Over-seriousness |

# The Aha Moment Stimulus

## The Gate of Realization

People who synthesize things together particularly "how" things come together from the past. The ener of making sense of how the story, visually, from the past comes together which stimulates an aha moment. This energy sorts through the snapshots in their mind to find the beginning, middle and end of the story. This energy is generally focused on sense making and growth.

**Keyword:** Magic

### HIGH EXPRESSION

- Growth Mindset
- Sense Making
- Allowing Possibility
- Inspiring
- Expects
- Solutions
- Trust
- Aha Moments
- Transformation

### LOW EXPRESSION

- Uselessness
- Failure
- Meaningless
- How Obsessed
- Confusion
- Negativity
- Forcing Answers & Epiphanies
- Hopeless
- Dogmatic
- Oppression

## The Voice of Gate 47

"Based on what I've read/studied, here's how it should be done."

### How This Gate Supports Others:

I support you in seeing the possibilities and solutions. I answer the question, "How can I expand?"

# The Aha Moment Stimulus

## Questions to Ask

- Do you have a growth mindset?
- How are you supporting your mindset?
- Do you perceive yourself as negative or positive? How can you look at things from a more positive perspective?
- What can you do to build a strong trust with your mind?
- How are you moving from a state of despair to one of hope?
- What are you doing to contend with the pressures of the How's?
- What creative activity can you do to help with your mental anxiety?
- Are you feeling defeated? If so why?
- What do you need to do in order to trust your mind more?
- Are you allowing yourself to expand?
- How would you describe your attitude?
- Are you allowing epiphanies to come into your world or are you trying to force it?
- Where does this image / clip / sequence belong? How does this make sense?
- What story of the past are you trying to piece together?

## Gate of Realizing

| Center | Mind | Repressive | Hopeless |
|---|---|---|---|
| Astro Sign | Virgo | Reactive | Dogmatic |
| Element | Earth | Victim Pattern | Your karma |

# The Sage /
# The Well of Wisdom

## The Gate of Depth -

The Fear of Inadequacy. The intuitive methodical knowing, resources, and depth that lies within to find a potential solution from the human experience in order to move the collective forward in the future. This energy is a well of never ending depth that is to be used methodically in order to be constantly renewed. The gate of depth & wisdom to come up with new solutions. The fear that the knowledge and depth will escape you.

**Keyword:** Introspection

### HIGH EXPRESSION

- Depth
- Wisdom
- Mastery
- Balanced Knowledge Acquisition
- Simplicity
- Resourceful
- Solution
- Mastery
- Mentor
- Prepared
- Naturally Talented

### LOW EXPRESSION

- Overprepared
- Frustration
- Comfort Zone
- Inadequacy
- Over complication
- Bland
- Inadequacy
- Unscrupulous
- No Experimentation
- Overly Prepared

## The Voice of Gate 48

*"I'm worried that when I go to speak the knowledge/words/depth won't be there."*

*"I am taking this course and I realize I could probably teach it even though I often feel like/fear I don't know enough."*

*"I should take one more course before I do my own."*

*"I should show up but I'm afraid I don't know enough / not expert enough."*

### How This Gate Supports Others:

I support you in seeing a new solution based on the depth of knowledge that I have. I answer the question, "What does it look like to come up with something new?"

# The Sage / The Well of Wisdom

## Questions to Ask

- How will you recognize that you know enough?
- Are you staying small and in your comfort zone out of fear of inadequacy/not knowing enough?
- How are you regularly connecting to your wisdom?
- What fear do you need to reckon with in order to gain confidence around your depth of knowledge?
- What is a nugget of wisdom you have recently gleaned?
- What relationships, projects and courses are superficial that you need to let go of?
- Can you see that this experiment will lead to a solution?
- Why can't you just do this instead of talk about it?
- Are you using your depth methodically and giving yourself a chance to be renewed? Are you honoring the simplicity that exists within the depth?
- Where do you have a depth of knowledge?
- How do you work with your fear of not knowing enough?
- How will you finally know that you have enough knowledge?

### Gate of Depth

| Center | Spleen | Repressive | Bland |
|---|---|---|---|
| Astro Sign | Libra | Reactive | Unscrupulous |
| Element | Air | Victim Pattern | Inadequacy |

# The Revolution Leader

## The Gate of Rejection – Revolution

The gate of revolution that drives the fear of rejection and the unpredictability of nature. The acceptance or rejection of principles based on the needs of the community. The need for revolution when the community's needs are not being met. The relationship agreement between two people. The Fear of Rejection because of one's beliefs. Nervousness over receiving support or not.

**Keyword:** Revolution

### HIGH EXPRESSION

- Revolution
- Rebirth
- Principles
- Transformation
- Never Settling
- What's Needed
- Communication
- Animal Connection

### LOW EXPRESSION

- Emotional Reactions
- Rejecting
- Rejection
- Struggling to Communicate
- Principles & Expectations
- Rejection of Self
- Quits Prematurely
- Insensitive
- Violence
- Killing

## The Voice of Gate 49

*"These are my values and I am not willing to compromise because this is what I believe."*

### How This Gate Supports Others:

I support you with my ability to uphold my principles and see the value in myself. I answer the question, "Who and what is needed in order to make _____ happen? Is this person no longer valuing me? What do I need to let go of in order to make space for transformation / revolution in order to live in alignment with a higher set of principles so that I can expand?"

# The Revolution Leader

## Questions to Ask

- What is your relationship like with resources? Do you trust because you have them now they will be available in the next moment?
- What are your principles?
- What is your relationship like with rejection?
- Is it time to hold your principles and start a revolution?
- Are you holding on too long?
- Are you holding on to a situation that you know is unhealthy because you fear the change that comes with it?
- Are you doing the work that it takes to create true emotional intimacy?
- What do you need to let go of to create room for you to align with your principles? What is your relationship like with quitting?
- What is your relationship like with your self-worth?
- Are you compromising your value for others?
- Are you in integrity with your principles?
- Are you willing to be rejected in order to uphold higher values?
- Whose support do you have?

## Gate of Principles

| Center | Solar Plexus | Repressive | Inert |
|---|---|---|---|
| Astro Sign | Aquarius | Reactive | Rejecting |
| Element | Air | Victim Pattern | Emotional reactions |

# The Caring Parent

## The Gate of Values –

The gate of values that drives the fear of caring too much or not enough. The awareness of being responsible for others in the community. An aura that takes responsibility or not. This is the gate of cooking and the bringing together/synthesis of ingredients/resources to develop and elevate a community. The fear of responsibility and environmental disharmony. Clarity on values is key.

**Keyword:** Evolution

### HIGH EXPRESSION

- Values
- Cooking
- Synthesizing
- Thriving
- Equilibrium
- Harmony
- Self – Care
- Challenge Standards & Norms
- Caring
- Guardian
- Trustworthiness
- Wellbeing
- Elevate

### LOW EXPRESSION

- Guilt
- Overloaded
- Irresponsible
- Environmental Disharmony
- Survival
- Mentality
- Not Caring For Oneself
- Caring for Wrong People
- No Evolution

## The Voice of Gate 50

"I know this is what is expected in terms of the values of society but I want to challenge that thinking because it is outdated."

### How This Gate Supports Others:

I support you with challenging your values and elevating your wellbeing. I answer the question, "What values might I need to reconsider in order to better nurture and nourish & elevate myself?"

# The Caring Parent

## Questions to Ask

- Do you have a clear sense of your values?
- Are you synthesizing your own values?
- Which values are a non-negotiable for you?
- How do you work with the guilt that you feel?
- What guilt do you need to let go of?
- Are you feeling guilty or free?
- Do you feel like you are failing others?
- How do you let go of the feeling of failing others?
- Are you being too rigid?
- What role does guilt play in your life?
- Are you letting guilt drive your decision making?
- Are you letting the fear of failing others drive your decision making?
- Are you over caring for others and failing to put yourself first?
- What actions are you taking out of obligation?
- Are you being overly judgmental or rigid with others? What is your relationship like with self-care?
- Are you prioritizing your own self-nourishment?
- Are you cooking your own food?
- How do you actually feel about putting yourself first?
- Are you taking responsibility for "stuff" that's not yours? What do you actually want to take responsibility for? What cause do you fight for and want to take action on?

## Gate of Values

| Center | Spleen | Repressive | Overloaded |
|---|---|---|---|
| Astro Sign | Libra & Scorpio | Reactive | Irresponsible |
| Element | Air - Water | Victim Pattern | Environmental disharmony |

# The Shocker / Early Adopter / Trend Setter

## Gate of Shock

The need to be first, best and/or shocking. People who are competitive by nature and want to be the best, first, and set the trend. People who are here to be catalysts for growth because they are early adopters. The energy of the individual initiative. The courage to be best or first.

**Keyword:** Initiative

### HIGH EXPRESSION

- Trendy
- Competitive
- Disruption
- Courageous Warrior
- Experience
- Initiative
- Adaption
- Growth
- Transcend of Ego
- Integration
- Catalysts
- Willpower

### LOW EXPRESSION

- Narcissistic
- Controlling
- Foolish Warrior
- Hostile
- Anxiety
- Aggravated
- Shocking just to Shock
- Withdrawn
- Lose Faith
- Lash Out
- Moving Quickly

## The Voice of Gate 51

"I am going to go do _____ (something extreme and shocking) because _____."

### How This Gate Supports Others:

I support you with my will to compete and be the first / best/ market disrupter. I answer the question, "Does this challenge to the status quo / innovate / disrupt? What do I need to do to be the best?

# The Shocker / Early Adopter / Trend Setter

## Questions to Ask

- What is your relationship like with competition?
- Do you do things just to be shocking?
- What happens when you aren't first?
- What have you learned from being shocking?
- What are you here to wake people up from?
- Are you connected to your true purpose in life?
- Have you transcended your ego or are you letting it run the show?
- What are you a catalyst of?
- Are you giving yourself time to integrate what you learned?
- What is your relationship like with control?
- Are you forging yourself in the fire of experience before you try and take control?
- Are you overly proving yourself and therefore giving your power away?
- Are you honoring the timing of your life?
- Are you in tune with what is ready to emerge to set a precedence, trend, or evolution?

Gate of Shock

| Center | Heart | Repressive | Cowardly |
|---|---|---|---|
| Astro Sign | Aries | Reactive | Hostile |
| Element | Fire | Victim Pattern | Anxiety |

# The Buddha

## The Gate of Stillness

The ability to slow down the body in order to concentrate on a project in order to gain perspective, a unique vantage point, or assessment for the betterment to gain insights. Stillness that drives the stress/pressure to focus your energy. One of the two ways to enter into stress properly is from a place of groundedness or joy (gate 58).

**Keyword:** Stillness

### HIGH EXPRESSION

- Stillness
- Assessment
- Empowerment
- Perspective
- Disciplined
- Restraint
- Hawk Eye Perspective
- Rising Above
- Clarity

### LOW EXPRESSION

- Frozen
- Overwhelmed
- Frantic
- Reactive
- Withdrawn
- Stuck
- Stressed
- Lazy
- ADHD
- Depression
- No Focus
- Antsy
- Restless
- Guilt

## The Voice of Gate 52

"I can get in the zone and focus for hours at a time."

"I feel this restlessness and tension in my body but I'm not sure what to focus on."

"I should try this new thing even though it might sabotage this other thing I'm working on"

### How This Gate Supports Others:

I support you in getting grounded in order to gain clarity. I answer the question, "How can I clear my mind, still my body, slow down in order to gain clarity on what is next?"

# The Buddha

## Questions to Ask

- What is worthwhile to concentrate on?
- Are you taking a temporary break from action in order to benefit your creative process?
- Are you honoring the tension/pressure you feel in your body to rest so that you can gain clarity on what to focus on?
- Are you giving yourself the space to see the bigger picture?
- Is the work that you are concentrating on meaningful and worthwhile?
- Have you taken time to assess what is worth focusing on?
- How can you channel your restless energy?
- Is it time to take a break to gain clarity?
- Are you busy being busy?
- What environment supports you in getting grounded and calm?
- How do you handle/cope with overwhelm?
- What can you do to better resource yourself so that you can manage overwhelm?
- What is the one thing you need to focus on in order to clear your path in order to move forward?
- How can you find more compassion toward yourself when you experience overwhelm/tension/franticness?

## Gate of Inaction

| Center | Root | Repressive | Stuck |
|---|---|---|---|
| Astro Sign | Cancer | Reactive | Restless |
| Element | Water | Victim Pattern | Stress |

# The Starter

## The Gate of Action

Drives the stress or pressure to start new things and begin. People who can leave food, projects and books unfinished. The energy to start lots of things but may struggle to finish. The energy of experience repeating because it got abandoned mid-way through or started prematurely.

### Keyword: Transformation

### HIGH EXPRESSION

- Beginnings
- Initiate Others
- Starting
- Expansion
- Honoring Cycles
- Initiations in Response
- Following Through
- Elevation

### LOW EXPRESSION

- Burnout
- Forcing
- Not Finishing
- Prematurely Starting
- Self-Criticism
- Feeling Like a failure
- Fickle
- Stress
- Pressure
- Repeating Cycles
- Guilt
- Shame
- Forcing

## The Voice of Gate 53

"I feel the pressure to start another project even though I have 4 more that I need to finish."

### How This Gate Supports Others:

I support you with my ability to start something new - creative endeavors, projects, learnings etc. I answer the question, "What should I initiate or start?"

# The Starter

## Questions to Ask

- Are you afraid to start something new because of failing in the past?
- What stories are you carrying about not finishing?
- Are you stuck in freeze mode because you are afraid if you start something new you will not finish?
- Are you honoring / trusting the timing of your life?
- Are you sharing / guilting / judging yourself for not finishing?
- Are you beating yourself up for having to start over again?
- What can you do to more fully trust the timing of your life?
- Are you forcing finishing and burning out?
- How can you have more compassion for yourself?
- Are you reacting to the pressure you feel instead of trusting the timing?
- Are you too afraid to start anything because you believe you won't finish?
- Do you even know what you want to start? What are you inspired by?
- Are you allowing your initiations to flow or are you forcing them?
- What is the lesson you learned from the cycle you just finished? Do you feel elevated and integrated before you start this new endeavor?

### Gate of Beginnings

| Center | Root | Repressive | Solemn |
|---|---|---|---|
| Astro Sign | Cancer | Reactive | Fickle |
| Element | Water | Victim Pattern | Inability to complete |

# The Ambitious Prosperity Seeker

## The Gate of Ambition

Drives the stress or pressure to achieve, transform, climb and be materially successful. The energy to ascend the hierarchy in pursuit of success, money, power or influence. Optimally it brings others with it as it achieves success.

**Keyword:** Ambition

### HIGH EXPRESSION

- Drive
- Ambition
- Ascension
- Entrepreneur
- Big Ideas
- Influence
- Greater Good
- Material Success
- Serving Others

### LOW EXPRESSION

- Burnout
- Deception
- Using Others
- Empty
- Greed
- Unambitious
- No Drive
- Lazy
- Over Ambitious
- Forcing
- Too Many Ideas
- Recognized
- Self-Serving

## The Voice of Gate 54

*"I hope that the CEO/Influencer notices all of the hard work that I've been putting in. I'm really hoping to get a promotion/contract."*

### How This Gate Supports Others:

I support you with my ambition, influence, and drive. I answer the question, "How can I achieve _____?"

# The Ambitious Prosperity Seeker

## Questions to Ask

- What do you need to do to work with your drive and ambition?
- Are you letting your drive dictate your action?
- Are you using your ambition for the good?
- What does material success mean to you?
- How much success is enough?
- What is your relationship like with your ambition and drive?
- What is your relationship like with getting credit for your ideas? Do you feel the need to prove it was your idea or do you believe you will be recognized?
- Who are you influencing in life?
- How do you contend with the pressure you feel to be successful?
- Are you forcing success?
- What is your relationship like with work? Are you working too hard?
- Which one of your ideas should you pursue?
- What does success mean to you?
- What is your definition of ambition?

## Gate of Ambition

| Center | Root | Repressive | Unambitious |
|---|---|---|---|
| Astro Sign | Capricorn | Reactive | Greedy |
| Element | Earth | Victim Pattern | Drive or lack of drive |

# The Spirited Artist

## The Gate of Spirit – Abundance

The gate of abundance that drives the desire to experience life through your passions and the fear of not knowing what to be passionate about to experience life to the fullest. The fear of emptiness. Nervousness over moods. The need to honor the moods that emerge within this energy so that it does n leave a wake of drama behind it.

**Keyword:** Abundance

### HIGH EXPRESSION

- Consciousness
- Trust
- Evolution
- Freedom
- Fullness
- Faith
- Surrender
- Support
- Spirit
- Passionate
- Honoring Moods
- Abundance
- Livelihood
- Artist
- Creative

### LOW EXPRESSION

- Indecisive
- Waffling
- Unaware
- Empty
- Fearful
- Complaining
- Drama
- Victim
- Moody
- Emotional Instability
- Melancholy
- No Passion
- Empty
- Anxious

## The Voice of Gate 55

*"I know that if I'm not in the mood to do x, it's just not going to happen."*

### How This Gate Supports Others:

I support people with finding the right state in order to create. I answer the question, "What practice do I need to cultivate to get into a creative flow? What can I do to deepen my trust that I will be able to tap into my creativity?"

# The Spirited Artist

## Questions to Ask

- Do you have faith and trust that things always work out for you?
- Where do you hold the doubt, fear and lack that you feel?
- Why do you carry that doubt, fear, and lack? How is it serving you?
- How are you connecting with the world around you and seeing the beauty, wonder and awe?
- Are you honoring your moods?
- Where have you left an emotional wake because of not being in the mood? Do you have language tracks prepared for when you are not in the mood? Do you have enough space in your day/life to honor your moods?
- How can you build a deeper trust in your ability to be emotionally aware? What is your relationship like with creativity?
- Do you feel like you live in an aligned manner?
- Are you connected to your muse?
- What limiting beliefs are you holding onto that are no longer serving you? Do you feel as though you are living in an aligned way?
- What is your relationship like with food?
- What is your relationship like with your moods?
- How are you using your emotional energy as a source of creative power?

## Gate of Spirit

| Center | Solar Plexus | Repressive | Complaining |
|---|---|---|---|
| Astro Sign | Pisces | Reactive | Blaming |
| Element | Water | Victim Pattern | Drama |

# The Wandering Story Teller

## The Gate of Stimulation - Stimulate

The Voice of I believe. These are people who love to tell stories and stimulate others through the stories they share – these stories may become exaggerated with each telling and may be stories from someone else's life. The expression of stories that enrich and teach the lives of the listeners.

**Keyword:** Stimulation

### HIGH EXPRESSION

- Storyteller
- Explorer
- Expansive
- Experience
- Enrichment
- Intoxicating
- Teacher
- Wanderer
- Beliefs
- Stability Through Movement

### LOW EXPRESSION

- Distraction
- Self-Judgement
- Excessive Exaggerations
- No one Interested
- Overstimulated
- Sullen
- Repelling
- No One Listening

## The Voice of Gate 56

"The other day, this client **** insert a story here**** did x and I honestly couldn't believe it. Do you believe it? Do you believe they were able to do x with know *** insert point of story****."

### — How This Gate Supports Others: —

I support you by sharing my stories in order to prove a point or illustrate a concept. I answer the question, "What story do I need to hear in order to see more possibility, growth or evolution?"

# The Wandering Story Teller

## Questions to Ask

- What stories do you regularly share and why?
- How can you add more spaciousness to your life in order to have more time to wander and collect experiences?
- Do you let your stories become too big?
- Are you "borrowing" other people's stories and asking permission?
- Are you judging yourself?
- Are the stories that you are sharing helping others see possibility and expand?
- Or are your stories spreading negativity?
- What narrative do you tell yourself that needs to change, adjust or be modified so that you can expand?
- Do you trust that the right people will be there for you to stimulate?
- Are you trying to live out all of the stories you are telling yourself?
- Are you telling stories from a place of despair or of hope?
- Do you allow yourself to wander and gain new experiences?
- Are you noticing how your own stories make you feel?

## Gate of Stimulation

| Center | Throat | Repressive | Sullen |
|---|---|---|---|
| Astro Sign | Cancer & Leo | Reactive | Over-stimulated |
| Element | Water – Fire | Victim Pattern | Distractions |

# The Intuitive

## The Gate of Intuitive Clarity

The Gate of intuition and instinct which hears the truth in the now via the right ear. Can have selective hearing. The fear of the future and unknown which can leave this energy in a holding pattern or indecis around what may happen next. This energy operates in the moment and must be present in order to he

**Keyword:** Instinct

### HIGH EXPRESSION

- Intuitive
- Instinctive
- Sensitive to Vibration
- Timing
- Self-Trust
- Survival
- Right Ear
- Alertness
- Clarity in the Now

### LOW EXPRESSION

- Fear of the Unknown
- Inaction
- Doubt
- Indecision
- Hesitant
- Impetus
- Frozen
- Fear Driven
- Half-hearted

## The Voice of Gate 57

*"I'm struggling to figure out what the future may hold for me. My vision is cloudy."*

*"I'm afraid of what the future may hold if I don't get clarity."*

### How This Gate Supports Others:

I support you with my intuitive hits and my instinctive knowing. I answer the question, "Do you have an knowing or instinct for me?"

# The Intuitive

## Questions to Ask

- Do you trust your instinct/Intuition?
- Are you honoring the timing of your life? Or are you second guessing everything?
- Are you emotionally sloppy?
- Are you fear mongering?
- Do you hear the intuitive nudge of this gate or is the not self of your mind chattering too loudly?
- What can you do to ground yourself in the moment?
- What practices do you need to quiet your mind?
- Do you recall a time when your instinct was correct, and you didn't honor it?
- Do you recall a time when your "instinct" was incorrect, and you honored it?
- What evidence can you muster up to prove to yourself that you can trust your intuition?
- Where in your life are you in indecision?
- What are you hesitant to move forward with?
- Do you trust the timing of your life?
- How can you reckon with your fear of the unknown?
- What can you do to build trust with this knowing?
- Where might you be silencing your gut response?
- What does your intuition / instinct feel like in your body?

## Gate of Intuitive Insight

| Center | Spleen | Repressive | Hesitant |
|---|---|---|---|
| Astro Sign | Libra | Reactive | Impetuous |
| Element | Air | Victim Pattern | Indecisions |

# The Delightful Spirit

## The Gate of Joy

Drives the stress or pressure to make better, correct and be of service. The stress of improvement. Peop[le] who have a zest / wonder for life and stop to take in the moment and enjoy it. They can see the potential in things and often correct what is out of alignment. One of two ways to enter into stress properly. From a place of joy.

**Keyword:** Joy

### HIGH EXPRESSION

- Zest for Life
- Magnetic
- Mastery
- Delight
- Joy
- Vitality
- Expression
- Bliss
- Love of Life
- Speculating
- Of Service
- Reach our Potential
- Wellbeing
- Aware

### LOW EXPRESSION

- Insatiable
- Perennially Dissatisfied
- Bitter
- Scrutinizing
- Critical

## The Voice of Gate 58

*"I feel the pressure to commit myself to a cause but I'm not sure exactly what I'm supposed to be working on."*

*"I see that we can improve this by doing x, y and z. If we improve that it will make the experience better for everyone."*

*"I should do this because x is already doing it and I have to keep up"*

*"I should be able to make this better/do this better/ be better."*

### How This Gate Supports Others:

I support you in spotting what needs to be corrected. I answer the question, "How can we improve upon this?"

# The Delightful Spirit

## Questions to Ask

- Are you satisfied in the now?
- How can you use the pressure of your unhappiness, discontent, dissatisfaction to trigger a transformation?
- What can you do to bring more joy into this moment?
- Why are you denying yourself joy and beauty?
- Are you afraid to do work you love?
- Is there a connection between your creative expression and your ability to manifest it in the physical world by leveraging joy?
- What can you do to find more joy in the moment?
- How can you move from dissatisfaction to joy?
- When was the last time you paused to revel in the wonder of the world?
- What brings you joy?
- What patterns are you noticing that are unhealthy?
- Where are you holding yourself back from experiencing joy and doing work you love? How are you sharing your talent with the world?
- Where do you need to add more repetitions in your work to curate and hone your talents?
- Where are you trying to hard to be of service?
- Where might your service orientation be received?

## Gate of Vitality

| Center | Root | Repressive | None |
|---|---|---|---|
| Astro Sign | Capricorn | Reactive | Interfering |
| Element | Earth | Victim Pattern | Ingratitude |

# The Intimate Creative

## The Gate of Sexuality/Intimacy

Drives the energy to bond, be intimate and create – frustration over boundaries and staying on the surface of true intimacy. The ability to break down walls in others often quickly. This energy needs to respond vs force intimacy.

**Keyword:** Dispersion

### HIGH EXPRESSION

- Intimacy
- Sexuality
- Transparency
- Vulnerability
- Creating & Sustaining humans or projects
- Fertility
- Aura Breaker
- Deep
- Legacy
- Dispersion

### LOW EXPRESSION

- Intrusive
- Excluded
- Judgement with Sexuality & Intimacy
- Defensiveness
- Anger
- Lack of Intimacy
- Jumping into Bonds Prematurely
- Surface Level

## The Voice of Gate 59

"I'm frustrated that x has stepped over the boundaries I laid it out."

### How This Gate Supports Others:

I support you with my ability to create and sustain people and business endeavors. I answer the question, "Is this sustainable and does it support the foundation I am building in life/biz? Who can I collaborate with?"

# The Intimate Creative

## Questions to Ask

- Do you know your role in creating relationships? Are you honoring that role?
- Do you feel safe to feel vulnerable?
- Are you penetrcting others unnecessarily?
- Who are you dancing with your penetrating aura?
- Are you forcing your rightness onto others unnecessarily?
- Are you letting fear and vulnerability hold you back from creating relationships? Are you trusting in the sustainability in your life?
- Do you have relationships and agreements that bring you energy or drain you? What is your relationships like with being right?
- Where has your rightness impacted relationships?
- Are you open to thinking in other ways?
- How do you create agreements with others?
- What values/perspectives are non-negotiables?
- Where are you creating unnecessary friction in your life?
- Are you creating peace or war with your approach to others?

Gate of Sexuality

| Center | Sacral | Repressive | Excluded |
|--------|--------|------------|----------|
| Astro Sign | Virgo | Reactive | Intrusive |
| Element | Earth | Victim Pattern | Relationships |

# The Resourceful Optimist

## The Gate of Acceptance - Limitation

The format energy of innovation that drives the stress or pressure to evolve and go beyond limitations. The need to surrender to the limits of what is present in order to innovate. When one surrenders innovation can emerge. When one resists one is often met with pressure.

**Keyword:** Limitation

### HIGH EXPRESSION

- Boundaries
- Resourceful
- Inventive
- Patient
- Accepting
- Tenacious
- Stillness
- Disciplined
- Accepting Limitation
- Realism

### LOW EXPRESSION

- Depression
- Stuck
- Restless
- Stressed
- Apathy
- Pressured
- Resisting
- Forcing Change
- Limited by Material Plane
- Negative

## The Voice of Gate 60

*"I feel a near constant pressure to bring something new into this world but I know if I'm patient my innovation will come at the right moment."*

### —How This Gate Supports Others:—

I support you with my ability to bring about lasting change in the world by understanding what works in the past. I answer the question, "what's working an how can I use that to innovate, invent or transform?"

# The Resourceful Optimist

## Questions to Ask

- What are you working on that is working?
- Do you see life through the lens of the glass half full or half empty?
- Do you feel creatively stuck?
- Where are you feeling resistance in your life?
- What are you holding on to that you need to let go of?
- Are you focusing on what isn't working?
- How do you deal with stress in your life?
- Is your fear holding you back?
- What resources are you working with while you tend to your idea?
- What is working? What is not?
- What is your relationship with change like?
- Are you afraid to let your new ideas emerge and disrupt? Or are you afraid to share
- them?
- Are you holding on instead of growing?
- Are you resisting change?
- Are you holding on to the old? Are you refusing to let go of the old?
- How can you better embrace change in your life?
- Do you feel creative paralysis?
- What letting go practices could you cultivate?
- Where do you need to surrender to the wave instead of resisting it?

## Gate of Acceptance

| Center | Root | Repressive | Unstructured |
|---|---|---|---|
| Astro Sign | Capricorn & Aquarius | Reactive | Rigid |
| Element | Earth - Air | Victim Pattern | Structures |

# The Truth Seeker

## The Gate of Mystery – Inner Truth

Contemplating the present – "Why" – Creative Inspiration. The mental pressure of resolving what is unknown, conceptualizing, and rationalizing. People who can rationalize almost anything for better or worse that has happened in the past.

**Keyword:** Conceptualizing

### HIGH EXPRESSION

- Epiphany
- Mystical
- Curious
- Knowing
- Inner Truth
- Rationalize
- Inspiration
- State of Wonder
- Calm Mind
- Wonder
- Awe
- Quiet
- Dreaming

### LOW EXPRESSION

- Endless Why
- Disenchanted
- Fanatical
- Obsessive
- Psychosis
- Madness
- Bored
- Pressured
- Controlling
- Manic
- Rationalizing Bad Behavior
- Delusional

## The Voice of Gate 61

*"I had this aha moment when I was reading this article and it totally helped me make sense of my project. I can finally feel like I know how I can bridge this stuff together."*

### How This Gate Supports Others:

I support you in contemplating "the why" of the present to spark creative inspiration. I answer the question –"Why did this happen? In order to be a catalyst for an epiphany"

# The Truth Seeker

## Questions to Ask

- What is your story?

- Who are you?

- How does it all work?

- What does it mean for you to get to your inner truth?

- What old beliefs, patterns and thoughts are you holding on to that you need to let go of? Are you trying to force wonder and aha's in your life?

- How do you stay connected to your sense of wonder?

- How can you build a better trust with your inner knowing?

- When do you question it? When do you trust it? What is your relationship with it like? What do you see on the horizon that offers a new perspective?

- How are you dancing with the near constant pressure that you feel?

- Where are you feeling frantic? Or melancholic?

- Where are you pressuring yourself?

- Are you working the voices in your head?

- Where might you need to put your mind to work instead of letting it run the show?

- How are you working with the melancholy you feel?

## Gate of Mystery

| Center | Head | Repressive | Disenchanted |
|---|---|---|---|
| Astro Sign | Capricorn | Reactive | Fanatical |
| Element | Earth | Victim Pattern | Obsessive mind |

# The Sense Maker /
# The Abstract Communicator

## The Gate of Details

The Voice of I think – People who can explain the intangible and make it understandable for the collective, while naming the details along the way. This gate is all about the expression of the details along the way. This is the ability to see and name the details/obstacles that may emerge.

**Keyword:** Nuance

### HIGH EXPRESSION

- Decisive
- Detailed
- Organized
- Articulate
- Methodical
- Naming
- Spotting
- Pitfalls
- Precision
- Impeccability
- Expressing Valuable Details
- Practical
- Organized

### LOW EXPRESSION

- Hung Up on Detail
- Too Stuck on Plan
- Fearful
- Worried
- Obsessive
- Vague
- Too much detail
- Stuck Pattern
- Limited to Logic

## The Voice of Gate 62

*"I think we could go one of the following ways. If we go this route then these things will come and if we go that route this may come up. And I can see either way this may happen."*

### How This Gate Supports Others:

I support you by providing certainty, naming and details of what might emerge on the path. I answer the question, "Could you explain _____? This is where I want to understand / go / learn more about."

# The Sense Maker /
# The Abstract Communicator

## Questions to Ask

- Do you have the facts that you need in order to use your voice?
- Are you overthinking the details before you get into action?
- Do you trust that have enough facts in order to move forward?
- Are you spending too much time prepping instead of being in the present moment?
- Are you sweating the details?
- Are you overly prepared, only following the plan on paper instead of trusting your intuition?
- Are you letting your worry drive your actions?
- Are you overly committed to the plan instead of striking a balance between the plan and the flow?
- Is your need to have a plan a, plan b, and plan c keeping you stuck?
- Are you completely overwhelmed by all of the details?
- What do you need to do in order to learn to find flow and trust in your knowing?
- How will you know when you've done enough preparation?
- Are you using excuses (over details, plans) to prevent yourself from moving forward?
- How is this pattern going to work before you present the facts/details?

### Gate of Detail

| | | | |
|---|---|---|---|
| **Center** | Throat | **Repressive** | Obsessive |
| **Astro Sign** | Cancer | **Reactive** | Pedantic |
| **Element** | Water | **Victim Pattern** | Language |

# The Inquisitor

## The Gate of Doubt

The doubts and suspicions to spot abstract mental patterns that are future focused and prompt a question. Securing the future – What? – Logical – The mental pressure of questioning, doubt, and needir an answer. This energy by nature is suspicious and questioning of the collective.

**Keyword:** Inquiry

### HIGH EXPRESSION

- Doubt
- Curiosity
- Decisive
- Truth
- Stimulating
- Validates Patterns
- Skeptical
- Questioning
- Self-Trust
- Proof

### LOW EXPRESSION

- Self-Doubt
- Suspicious
- Proof Seeking
- Non-Questioning
- Inadequate
- Doubt
- Questions
- Suspicious
- Distrust
- Dreamkiller

## The Voice of Gate 63

*"I have so many questions that I can't seem to find answers for and I really need an answer.."*

*"I should be able to do this but I don't think I know how."*

*"I should be able to trust x but I'm going to need to see proof first."*

### How This Gate Supports Others:

I support you in spotting the logic and patterns of what might emerge in the future. I answer the question, What do we need to be mindful of in the future?

# The Inquisitor

## Questions to Ask

- If you are suspicious or doubtful about x what details do you need to prove to yourself that you can let go of that pressure?
- Do the people, places or things in your life make you feel suspicious? If so, why? What can you do to prove to yourself you can let go of that doubt around them?
- Are you remaining composed in spite of your doubt and suspicions? Or are you letting your suspension run your life?
- Are you letting your suspicions hold you back?
- Are you holding on to your suspicions and doubts instead of realizing you have the answer?
- Are you dancing with your doubts?
- How can you prove to yourself that the people/things in your life are proven? What details do you need to let go of the suspicions?
- How can you work with your self-doubt in a way that supports you moving forward?
- Are you certain that this is for you?
- How are you using your curiosity to spark and stimulate new ideas?
- What do you need to do to feel certain that you can trust your ideas?
- How can you work with your own self-doubt? How can you resource yourself so that it doesn't cripple you?
- What are you curious about?
- How can you substantiate your claims? What proof or facts do you need?

Gate of Doubt

| Center | Head | Repressive | Self doubt |
|---|---|---|---|
| Astro Sign | Pisces | Reactive | Suspicion |
| Element | Water | Victim Pattern | Doubts |

# The Dreamer

## The Gate of Confusion –

Make Sense of the past "how" – Abstract Visual – The mental pressure to resolve the past and the confusion of how it will make sense. This energy has an intensity to it which is here to figure out how something is possible.

**Keyword:** **Possibilities**

### HIGH EXPRESSION

- Possibilities
- Inspiration
- Vision
- Aha's Imagination
- Illumination
- Big Picture
- Epiphanies
- Past
- Sense Making
- Figuring out the "how"
- Passage
- Intensity

### LOW EXPRESSION

- Idea Overwhelm
- Stuck in How
- Pressure
- Despair
- Overly Sense making
- Imitating
- Confusion
- Mental Anxiety
- Giving Up
- Can't Handle Mental Pressure
- Stuck in How

## The Voice of Gate 64

*"I am a very visual person. My mind is always flooded with images of my past, and it makes me confused. I just want it to make sense."*

*"I should be able to bring this big idea to fruition but I don't feel adequate/enough."*

*"I should be able to figure out this solution but...."*

### — How This Gate Supports Others:—

I support you in making sense of the past by visually finding patterns in the world. I answer the question, – how does this all make sense?

# The Dreamer

## Questions to Ask

- Are you allowing the information and mental pressure to pass through you without resistance?
- How are you honoring the many ideas that emerge in your mind?
- Are you allowing your overwhelm to discourage you and give up on your dreams?
- Are you staying in the possibilities and dreams?
- Are you worrying about the how?
- Are you honoring the timing of life to allow for sense making to happening or are you rushing?
- What do you need to do in order to work with the confusion that you feel?
- How are you working with the pressure of your mind instead of resisting it?
- What does it look like to allow yourself to dream and be in the possibilities?
- Which ideas are mine to take action on? And which do you need to let go of?
- Are you feeling inadequate and ungrounded?
- What can you do to resource yourself to relieve the pressure and confusion of your mind?

## Gate of Confusion

| Center | Head | Repressive | Imitating |
|---|---|---|---|
| Astro Sign | Virgo | Reactive | Confused |
| Element | Earth | Victim Pattern | Confusion |

# Gates Themes Distilled

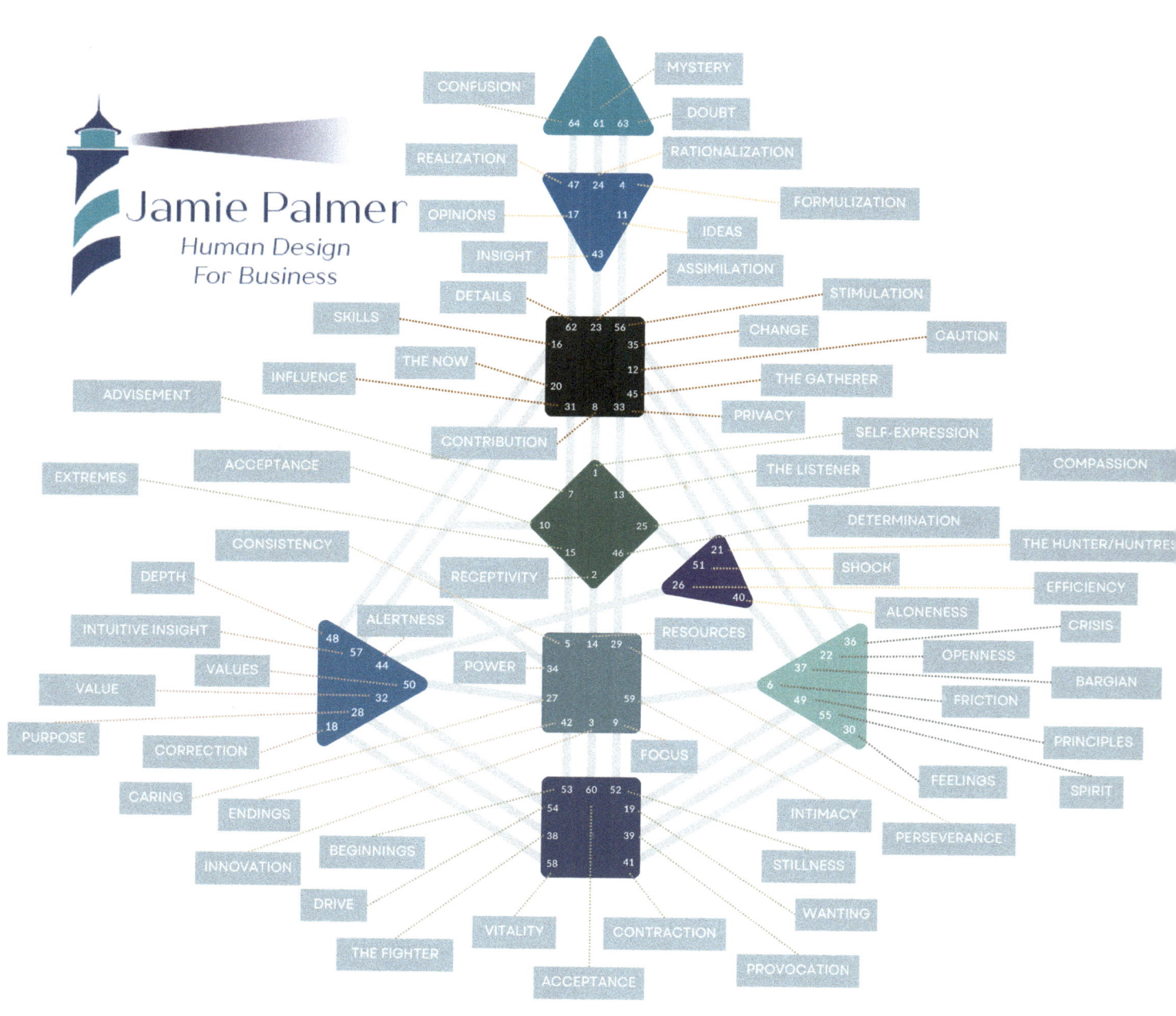

A digital copy of this is available on the learning platform when you download
the additional resources at hdgatestrengths.com

# About the Author

Jamie Palmer has over nearly 20 years advising and supporting businesses across the spectrum of experience and expertise — from small mom and pop shops and digital solopreneurs to over $10 million a year business owners and brick and mortar businesses and restaurateurs. She bridges her business insight and experience with her human design depth and penetrating insight to fuse and create a new form of business guidance leveraging the human design system for business owners all around the world. She currently works with business owners and students in over 40 countries, making her reach and work global.

With a unique ability to take a hawk-eye view and her fearless need to explore the depths, evolve, and push the boundaries of what is established and known, Jamie is on a mission to innovate and liberate you from the false beliefs, ideas, and inner and outer obstacles that hold you back in your life and business so you can truly build a life and business you love. Starting her first business in her twenties, Jamie has cultivated a diverse ecosystem of knowledge and expertise, synthesized into the revolutionary system known as Ecocentric Human Design - which includes the following programs, Business Design with Human Design, the program to create your business model by design; HD Your Biz, a set of programs to build your sales, marketing, messaging, and more leveraging human design; and HD in the Wild, the training program for business owners looking to revolutionize their industry by leveraging the human design system to pioneer and create their own unique perspectives, individualized client services, products, and programs, and HD-informed systems and expertise.

# About the Author

Jamie is known for her ability to make human design practical, digestible, and instantly knowable. You can see this through her following and resources shared on Instagram, her podcast, and blogs, as well as her many accessible resources on her site. She makes human design accessible in many ways by looking at and creating programs that teach and leverage the whole system and entirety of one persons' design, and not just looking at a surface level solution or advice for how people should design their life and businesses.

Jamie believes that your voice is important and essential to a future where we can thrive, not only as individuals but also connected to the beauty of a sustainable world and ecosystem. She firmly believes that your success doesn't have to cost the earth. All of this has led her to appreciate sustainability on many levels and embrace the philosophy of doing more with less. Her unique approach to human design is based on an ecosystem and whole system view, and teaches business owners how to leverage their human design to build a business and life that is sustainable and self generating for years to come. The intention for all her programs and resources is to build a resource you can return to over the course of your life and business.

Jamie's first book, Human Design for Business book is one of many to come from her unique perspective and application of making human design practical, accessible, and relevant for business owners world wide. In her own life, Human Design has completely transformed her own business and world by changing how she parents, how she takes care of and understands herself, and by giving her permission to create success in a radically new way — on her own terms. Her hope is that human design can light the same spark and fire for you, and create that opening for you to revolutionize your business and life, too.

When not creating Human Design programs or coaching, Jamie can be found in Newport, RI, with her kiddos and husband hanging out in nature, paddleboarding, writing, or turning her backyard into an edible landscape.

Jamie's passions have led her in many directions. All of this has led her to appreciate sustainability on many levels and embrace the philosophy of doing more with less.

If you are ready to free your voice and create impact, Jamie can steward you to fulfillment.

# Resources & Additional Support

The HD Your Biz Show podcast—My weekly podcast diving into all things Human Design, business, and living life in high definition.

The Blog—My blog is a great place to dive deeper into different aspects of Human Design.

The Impact Sphere—A community for people who want to live life and business in high definition using their Human Design.

Ideal Client Workshop —Discover your ideal client by design with this proprietary process to magnetize your ideal client with more ease and consistency using your human design www.idealclientdesignwithhumandesign.com.

The Line Experience - Audio Deep Dive - Delve into the 6 lines which make up the 12 profiles in human design to better understand the congruence compass, attachments  styles, social and emotional IQ, ideal role and more. www.humandesignlineexperience.com

Business Design With Human Design—If you want to learn how to create an offer in congruence with your Human Design, this course is a great way to know which aspects of your design to look at. We dive into centers, variables, circuitry, and more when deciding what elements to include in your offer, your transformation promise, and how you attract clients: www.businessdesignwithhumandesign.com.

HD Your Biz®—The 16 Week Program to HD Your Business and Life. If you want to dig deeper into strategy, branding, marketing, sales, storytelling, productivity, tech, and leadership by design, I invite you to join me on this journey: www.hdyourbiz.com.

HD Wild®— Human Design Certification Program - Create a blue ocean in your industry and get certified in Ecocentric Human Design®. If you want to incorporate Human Design into your existing expertise while getting support for your business, this is the program for you. This is a one-year, high-touch program to learn Human Design, develop your own intellectual property with this tool, and get support for living your design. I invite you to dive into the wild world of Human Design with me: www.hdinthewild.com.